WHO ARE THESE PEOPLE, AND WHAT HAVE YOU DONE WITH MY PARENTS?

WHO ARE THESE PEOPLE, AND WHAT HAVE YOU DONE WITH MY PARENTS?

KELLY HYMANYK

MEGAMY

THE PUBLISHER:
Megamy Publishing Ltd.
P. O. Box 3507
Spruce Grove, Alberta, Canada T7X 3A7
E-mail: megamy@interbaun.com

National Library of Canada Cataloguing in Publication

Hymanyk, Kelly, 1963-
   Who are these people & what have you done with
my parents?/
Kelly Hymanyk.

ISBN 978-0-9733728-3-0

   1. Grandparent and child- -Humor. I. Title.
II. Title: Who are these people and what have you done
with my parents?.

PN6231.G8H94 2006   306.874'50207   C2006-902659-9

Copy Editor: Natalie King
Design, layout, and production: Kelly Hymanyk and Robert Adams
Cover: NEXUS Design
Printing: McCallum Printing Group Inc.

AUTHOR'S NOTE

About thirteen years ago I had the opportunity to go to a small, informal Girl Guide reunion. I had been a Girl Guide for a number of years in my teens. I had made great friends while participating in the guiding experience. —I had gone on numerous camping trips in Alberta and Montana with my troop and I was excited to see some of these women from my past, most of whom I had not seen for at least fifteen years.

During the reunion we reminisced about our adventures as Girl Guides, and what struck me most that evening was that although we had shared the same experiences, —going to the same camps, playing the same pranks, singing the same songs— we all remembered different things, or the same things in different ways, or at least different parts of the same things. In fact, our memories were so different that I sometimes got the feeling we had not shared the same experience at all.

It is with that in mind that I have approached the writing of this book. These are my memories of my youth, of my parents in the early years, and of our experiences together.

A big thank you to my parents, Bob and Martha, who have such a good sense of humour about the way I remember the early years. I will always love you, and I am grateful for your unwavering support throughout my life.

CONTENTS

INTRODUCTION

Join Hymanyk as she happily embarks on the fabulous journey known as parenthood.

Laugh as she tries to come to grips with her parents, her children's grandparents who have suddenly changed before her very eyes. The two most important people from her childhood, who she remembers as being rational and logical, while she was being raised. Frugal, conservative people, possessing a strong sense of right and wrong.

With the birth of her first child, Hymanyk looked on in disbelief as everything she had been taught disappeared, vanished into thin air like a wisp of cloud.

The rational, logical parents she knew changed, and overnight she found herself in a world she was not prepared for. Not only did the rules change, but there was a new rule for every situation and never the same rule twice.

Hymanyk takes the reader on this wild hilarious journey sharing her unique sense of humour that helps her cope with her parents, her children's overindulgent grandparents. A must read for all.

MEGAMY PUBLISHING

WHO ARE THESE PEOPLE,
AND WHAT HAVE YOU
DONE WITH MY PARENTS?

WHO ARE THESE PEOPLE, AND WHAT HAVE YOU DONE WITH MY PARENTS?

Sometimes I look at my parents, the grandparents of my children—Nanna and Pa, as we lovingly call them now—and I think, Who are these people? What has happened to my parents? They certainly are not the same people who were responsible for my child-rearing. They are definitely not the people I saw in the rear-view mirror when I left home to go to university. I mean, physically they look like my parents, but something is definitely not right.

My mother and father were serious people. They worked long hours and had little time to play.

Nanna and Pa are always happy and more than willing to play. In fact, on most occasions they are the instigators of the good times. The words "no" and "not now I'm tired" have disappeared from their vocabulary. Not to mention that the purse strings have loosened up a lot. It's not like in the old days, when Mom and Dad had deep pockets and short arms.

Whatever happened to my parents' theory, "Work hard for something, and then you'll appreciate it more when you get it"? Or their belief that "You aren't entitled to something just because everyone else has one"? Nanna and Pa seem to be working with a new philosophy, a whole new set of rules—or should I say a complete lack of rules, for, amazingly, since my children were born, anything goes.

This was not what I was expecting from my parents. My parents are logical, rational people. Not only did they understand the need for rules and boundaries; they *made* the rules and were very good at enforcing them. At least, they used to be.

As difficult as it is to believe, it's a fact that with the birth of my children—Nanna and Pa's grandchildren—we instantly began playing a whole new game. As a player in that game, I, the parent, find myself in a most unenviable position. I appear to be the only one who has to learn the rules in order to be a contributing team member. However, learning the rules and being a contributing team member is an impossibility. I continually find myself alone out in left field, because the rule-makers keep making up the rules as they go along: a new rule to match every situation, and not necessarily the same rule in the same situation.

Sometimes in the beginning we're playing a friendly game of chess. I move my pawn one square straight ahead. Nanna and Pa countermove by sliding their pawn across the entire board, jumping over my king and taking out my queen. I start to explain to them that the pawn cannot move in just any direction, and certainly not ten spaces at a time. However, before I can finish my explanation, I find myself alone on the board. My playmates have moved on to the next game.

I struggle to catch up, and suddenly I'm on a large football field and I'm running a play from the playbook. This is a game I know very well; I have always been good at football. I enthusiastically join in. I'm running full speed down the field, and quite unexpectedly I find myself lying face up on the field, looking up at the sky spinning overhead—someone has clotheslined me. No flag on the play, no whistle, no penalty. It's then that I realize they knew which play I was running. Nanna and Pa have a copy of my playbook. In fact, I realize now, it's the playbook they wrote while I was growing up and they were my parents. Only now they're not reading their own plays; they're making up their plays as they go along. The quarterback is calling the game from the field.

Except that he's not a quarterback. He's a goalie from a hockey team, and he's passing to a tennis player who has a wicked backhand, and he's slamming the ball back over the net—which is really something to see, because that ball is a bowling ball.

It's at this moment that I realize the game is all mixed up. There are too many players on the field, and they aren't all playing the same game. And there are no rules—at least, none that I can figure out.

I'm certainly not an expert on sports by any means, but I do know that every game has a set of rules; you play with specific equipment, on a predetermined playing field. You must have these things in the world of sports, or there would be chaos.

Well, in the world of grandparenting, apparently, there are no rules; and so it would appear that anything goes. Nanna and Pa and my children are all having a ball. They're running and playing, oblivious to the chaos they're creating on the field. They're laughing and having a great time.

I want to scream, Be a sport! Give me a chance!

I struggle to get up, to pull my aching back up off the turf where I have been unceremoniously trampled. I plead with the team to include me. I want to run and jump and have fun too. I want to be on the team. To be one of the players.

"Play fair!" I cry out.

Sadly I realize that no one is listening. Not Nanna, not Pa, and certainly not my children, because it's almost time for supper, I am alone on the field, and they've all gone for ice cream.

Welcome to my world.

YOU'LL HAVE TO HOLD IT

"I really need to go to the bathroom, Pa," Amy said to her grandfather, squirming in her car seat as she attempted to hand her dad the dripping remains of her double-scoop ice cream cone to finish off.

Amy had barely made a dent in the two softball-size ice cream scoops before she was full and the ice cream started to melt. She was having trouble leaning far enough out of her car seat for a successful hand-off, and ice cream was dripping down the cone, over her hand, and onto the floor of the van.

It was certainly no surprise to me that she needed to go to the bathroom. We were only three hours into our holiday trip, heading from Edmonton to the interior of British Columbia, and already we

17

had stopped twice for treats along the way.

Our first pit stop had been in Red Deer's "gasoline alley" for drinks. Nanna and Pa let the girls out of the van to stretch their legs and then took them into the store to look at all the soft drinks and choose their favourites. Our second stop had been in Cochrane for giant scoops of Cochrane's world-famous ice cream. Again, the girls went with Nanna and Pa to decide what they would like. On an outing with Nanna and Pa the girls were allowed to have whatever they wanted—a cone, a milkshake, a sundae, anything that was on the menu. There were so many flavours that it had taken them quite a while to choose, but Nanna and Pa had waited patiently; it appeared that we were in no rush to arrive at our destination.

I had suggested that we pack a picnic lunch to eat along the way, but it seemed that packed lunches were a thing of the past for my parents. They kiboshed the planned picnic lunch in favour of the spontaneity of roadside restaurant visits.

"Amy, you should have gone to the bathroom when we were in Cochrane five minutes ago," I said. "It will be at least half an hour before we come to another rest area with a bathroom. It could even be longer; I haven't driven on this road for a long time."

The words were barely out of my mouth when I

felt the car slowing and heard the ticking of the flashing signal light. Apparently we were turning off the highway onto a little paved side road.

"Why are we stopping, Dad?" I asked.

It was not like my father to make unexpected stops at the side of the highway.

"We're not stopping. I'm just turning around to head back to Cochrane," he replied.

"Why would we do that?" I asked.

"Well, I haven't driven this road for a few years either, and I think you might be right—a rest stop could be a long way off. We'd better get this little girl back to Cochrane, where she can use the washroom," he said as he signalled again and drove back onto the highway in the direction we had just come.

"You're kidding," I said, and I'm sure my jaw dropped in disbelief.

I was, to say the least, a little stunned at this turn of events. As I looked at the back of my father's head from my vantage point in the middle of the van, I thought to myself, Who are you, and what have you done with my father? It was at that moment that car trips from my childhood came reeling back into my mind.

*   *   *   *   *

Sprawled in the back seat, as any lone child in the

seventies would be, I was free to move around, unrestricted by a seatbelt. The seatbelt laws were not to come into effect until years later; and apparently I was part of the generation that believed it wasn't dangerous to go without your seatbelt until law enforcement started giving you tickets for not wearing them.

With my pillows, blankets, and *Archie* comics I would wile away the long journey, perfecting my impersonation of a sloth—doing not much of anything.

"How long until we get there, Dad?" I asked. The tone in my voice carried a sense of urgency. "Can we stop for a break?" It seemed to me that we had been driving for a really long time.

"We're almost there," Dad replied.

"Bob!" my mom said, giving my dad an I-can't-believe-you-said-that look.

The look told me we were nowhere near *there,* wherever *there* was. But I had heard those words on every car trip we had ever taken. My dad hated to stop when he was on his way to somewhere, anywhere. I'm not sure if it's a guy thing or just my dad's little quirk, but for some reason stopping seemed to imply failure. Failure at what I had no idea.

"Do we need to stop for gas?" I asked, hoping the

answer would be "yes", but knowing that the answer would be "no".

"Nope," Dad stated.

"I need to go to the bathroom," I said.

"Well, you should have gone before we left," said Dad.

"I did go before we left. That was, like, days ago," I said, exaggerating to emphasize my point.

"We're almost there. You'll have to hold it," Dad said, putting an end to the conversation with his stand-pat answer.

It seemed like days since we had crossed the Alberta–Saskatchewan border. The gently rolling hills of the eastern Alberta prairies had faded in the distance—as had the smooth highway, which had come to an abrupt halt at the border. We found ourselves bouncing along a narrow road that appeared to have been paved only around the potholes. The rough road jarred my insides violently and added to my discomfort.

"I really have to go to the bathroom, Dad," I said again.

"Cross your legs and hold it," he replied.

"I am crossing my legs, and it isn't helping," I complained.

We made this trip across the prairies at least once a year when we headed back to Saskatchewan for our annual summer holiday at the farm. I loved the Saskatchewan countryside that whizzed past in the late summer. My favourite part was the endless wheat fields. On a bright, sunny day the blue sky accented the golden fields of wheat swaying in the prairie breeze. I liked it when a gust of wind caught the wheat and the whole field seemed to flow in waves. It was calming to watch wave after wave drift across the field until each disappeared over the horizon.

Yes, the Saskatchewan countryside just before harvest was magnificent, but all too often its beauty was lost on me. I had more pressing things on my mind. I had to go the bathroom in a big way. I was getting tired of having to suspend my bodily functions every year for these trips back to Saskatchewan; and for every other road trip we ever took, for that matter. I was sure that I was doing some irreversible damage to myself. I distinctly remember reading about a woman who held her pee so long that her bladder burst, and she died because the urine contaminated all her other internal organs. At least, I think I read about that; or it might have been one of those urban legends that someone told me about. Either way, I had a pretty vivid picture in my mind right then of my internal organs drowning as the urine gushed out of my burst bladder and into my body cavity.

"I really, really have to go to the bathroom, Dad," I begged for the third time.

"I told you, cross your legs and hold it," Dad said again.

"I did cross my legs, and I crossed my fingers too, but I still have to go to the bathroom."

What exactly did "hold it" mean, anyway? It's not as if there was really anything to hold. It would be like telling someone who was filling a glass of water to not let it overflow while you just kept pouring more water into the glass. I mean, logic tells you that when something is full, it's full. But year after year, road trip after road trip, Dad refused to stop and let me pee.

I tried to concentrate on something else, anything else. I watched the wheat fields whiz by, seemingly going on forever, taunting me, as if to say: You will never get to your destination. You will never pee again.

I pressed my face up against the glass of the closed window in an effort to distract myself. It didn't work. I watched the white lines on the road. I focused my energy on the little white lines, all the while pulling strands of my hair out of my mouth. My long, curly hair was blowing wildly in the wind that was whipping in from the two front windows that were rolled right down, directing gales of wind into the back seat as the car sped down the highway.

Those were the days when only the privileged few had air conditioning in their vehicles. The rest, people like my father, just let the wind whip through the interior of our cars, unconcerned with the tangles that would be knotted in our hair for days. When I say *our* hair, I mean of course all of us eleven-year-olds on vacation, riding in the back seat of the family car, continually being windblown so that the rest of the passengers could remain relatively cool. Occasionally I would ask for the windows to be rolled up, just for a reprieve from the wind. But no one was rolling up the window to swelter in the heat of a car at the request of the windblown child in the back seat.

Neither the white lines nor pulling the hair from my mouth worked. I still had to go. The sensation of the full bladder was becoming more urgent. I really need to pee, I thought, as I watched the little white lines flick by and fade into a blur. I needed more than the white lines to help me think of something else. I needed something that would be a complete distraction, maybe even distracting enough to encourage my dad to stop the car. Food was always a good direction to take with my dad. He loved his food.

"Are we going to stop for lunch?" I questioned, keeping my fingers crossed and praying for a "yes".

"No," Dad said.

"I brought a packed lunch. Would you like a sandwich?" my mom chimed in, happy to be changing the subject. I watched as she reached into the back seat to retrieve a huge brown bag that contained our lunch.

"I've got ham-and-cheese sandwiches," she said, and she produced a sandwich from the bag. "How does a nice ham-and-cheese sandwich with a little bit of mustard sound?"

"Mustard's gross," I said.

"Well, I can take the mustard off," Mom said as she began the process of carefully opening the sandwich. First she balanced the two sides of the bun precariously on her knees. One side of the bun was home to a slice of processed cheese and a thin slice of deli ham, the kind that comes prepackaged in the meat section of the grocery store. A small bit of mustard was dabbed on top of the slice of ham; the other side of the bun was saturated with what had once been a big glob of mustard.

"Hand me the Kleenex box," Mom said.

I reached down and carefully felt around the

floor of the back seat and underneath the front seat, finally producing the beat-up Kleenex box that was always kicking around in the car.

"Do you want the whole box?" I asked.

"No, just one Kleenex should do," Mom replied.

I passed one Kleenex forward, and without missing a beat Mom took the Kleenex and began wiping the mustard from the ham and the bun. The mustard came off the ham fairly well, but Mom was not very successful in removing the mustard from the bun itself. Try as she might, the mustard would not be sucked from the bun that had absorbed it like a sponge. Finally she gave up. She slapped the two halves of the bun back together, completely burying the ham and cheese, and handed it back to me.

"There you go," she said. "No mustard."

I stared at the sandwich in disbelief. I was tempted to tell her I had lost my appetite, that she was more than welcome to eat my sandwich herself. Who would want a ham-and-cheese-and-bits-of-Kleenex sandwich? But I knew better than to ask. We did not waste food in the Adams family. No sir, if you asked for it, you ate it. And although technically I had not asked for the sandwich that was now garnished with Kleenex fuzz, I knew it was considered to be mine, Kleenex and all.

I looked at the sandwich, closed my eyes, and took a big bite, stuffing at least a quarter of the sandwich into my mouth. I waited for the taste of Kleenex to filter through to my taste buds. But the taste of Kleenex was overpowered by the disgusting taste of mustard. I tried to chew faster. The taste was killing me and, to make matters worse, the dry bun was getting balled up in the back of my throat. I wasn't sure which was going to make me throw up first—the taste of the mustard or the huge clump of dough lodged in the roof of my mouth.

"Yuk, this sandwich is really dry," I said to my mom in a muffled voice.

"That's because you didn't want any mustard on it," Mom replied.

Yeah, I thought to myself sarcastically, that must be it.

"Well, now I need something to drink, please," I said, trying to hold back the gag reflex.

"I have tea in the Thermos," she said.

She took the lid off the Thermos and poured some tea into it. The lid doubled as a cup; this was really well thought out on the part of the Thermos people. It was even more clever if you were the sole owner of the Thermos and you could have the little cup all to yourself. In my family you shared the cup with everyone who wanted a hot drink, so it was always best to have the first drink, before anyone else, like Dad, contaminated his tea with sugar.

"Careful, it's hot," Mom said.

I gulped the tea down, burning my tongue and the roof of my mouth, but I didn't care just then. The liquid had the desired effect; it softened the sandwich so that I could chew it, and it also washed away some of the mustard taste. I finished off the sandwich, washing down the bun, the ham, the cheese, the mustard, and the mangled Kleenex with the tea, which had quickly cooled in the plastic lid.

"I can cut you up an apple if you'd like," Mom said when I had finished the sandwich.

I figured the apple might help to get rid of the lingering taste of mustard.

"Okay," I said.

Mom pulled out her little paring knife and started cutting up the apple into little wedges. I wondered, with a bit of disappointment, why my mom had never learned her mom's technique of peeling the skin off the apple in a single spiralling cut. The apple always tasted so much better when my grandma cut off the skin in one graceful motion. I ate a few slices of the apple that Mom passed back.

It wasn't long before I realized that drinking the tea had been a huge mistake. My need to go to the bathroom was even greater than it had been before.

"Dad, I have to go to the bathroom really bad," I said. "I don't think I can hold it any more. I'm going to pee my pants."

"For heavens sake, Bob, stop and let Kelly go to the bathroom," my mom said, finally coming to my rescue. "It will only take a minute."

"Well, there are no truck stops along here. She'll have to pee in the ditch," countered my dad.

"Ah, come on, Dad," I begged. "There must be a truck stop or restaurant coming up."

But my pleas fell on deaf ears, because as I was speaking the car was slowing down and inching over onto the narrow shoulder of the Saskatchewan highway. When we came to a complete stop, we were hanging off the side of the road with most of the car leaning over into the ditch.

"Well, there you go," Dad said, looking into the back seat. "Hurry up. We don't have all day."

"Dad, the other cars driving by can see me peeing in the ditch," I stated.

I knew this was an argument I would never win. If I wanted to pee, this would be my chance. Pee in the ditch or don't pee at all. This was nothing new. I had been peeing in ditches all over Saskatchewan, Alberta, and British Columbia for as long as I could remember. I would be hard pressed to think of a car trip when I hadn't at some point peed in a ditch.

29

Saskatchewan ditches were always the worst, because there were no trees to hide behind and the people in the other vehicles could see you for what seemed like forever.

Ditch-peeing had been less humiliating when we owned a four-door car. Then I could open the front and back door and brilliantly screen myself from both directions of traffic. Our two-door car always left me exposed to the traffic from one direction.

As I exited the vehicle, I opened the passenger door as wide as it would go. From my vantage point beside the car it seemed that even a slight wind might tip the car over into the ditch and on top of me. How humiliating that headline would be: GIRL DIES IN DITCH VICTIM OF TIPPING CAR. Or worse: GIRL PINNED BENEATH TIPPED CAR EXPOSED TO ONCOMING TRAFFIC PANTS AROUND ANKLES. I secretly prayed that the car would not tip over onto me as I squatted beside it.

I strategically placed myself in front of the door, screening myself from traffic heading in the same direction as we were, as well as from the other occupants of our vehicle. However, that did leave me in plain view of oncoming traffic. I quickly dropped my drawers and carefully squatted down, trying to avoid any plant life that might poke me.

Now, the most time-consuming step in ditch-peeing is the drip-dry. You can't use a tissue, as there is nowhere to dispose of it. The drip-dry always leaves you exposed a little longer than is comfortable. Occasionally some passersby will honk just to let you know they have witnessed your ditch squat. Some truckers seem to revel in your humiliation by giving a long blast on their air horn. The shock is enough to make the novice ditch-squatter topple over.

Luckily, on this particular day I was quick and avoided the next wave of oncoming traffic. I quickly made my way back into the vehicle, and we were off. I'm sure we had lost no more than two minutes of precious travel time.

Once on the road again, it was only a matter of minutes before we drove by the next truck stop fully equipped with public washrooms, but we blew by with no need to stop. I'm sure Dad knew that truck stop was there and made the conscious choice to make me pee in the ditch instead of stopping at the fully equipped facility. Maybe he thought we would lose too much time if I were allowed to dilly-dally in a public washroom.

Why couldn't we be like other families, I wondered, and pull in at a truck stop along the highway? We could even eat real food, restaurant food, and sit comfortably on real chairs at a table where we could enjoy our meal. Each of us could order what we wanted, and the choices would be more than mustard or no mustard. We could have a leisurely lunch that would be followed by a visit to the bathroom before we all piled back into the car to be on our way.

I knew that people ate at restaurants instead of packing a lunch, because there were always cars parked outside the restaurants at truck stops. And not just truckers. Why, I even knew families who ate at restaurants whenever they were on vacation.

What I didn't know way back in the seventies was that my time to pee at rest stops along the highway and eat restaurant food en route to a holiday destination with my father would come. I would just have to wait until his grandchildren were born. Thank heavens for the grandchildren; I don't relish the thought of having to squat and bare my butt in a Saskatchewan ditch at age forty.

Grandparents are similar to a piece of string—handy to have around and easily wrapped around the fingers of their grandchildren.

-Author Unknown

THE BROWN BIKE

"Which one do you like, Megan?" Nanna asked.

Megan, Nanna, and I were spending our Saturday afternoon at United Cycle. Nanna had decided that Megan needed a new bike. She was going into Grade Seven and she needed an appropriate bike to carry her to junior high school. Nanna wanted Megan to have something that was in style, something that would help her fit in. Nanna knew that the junior-high years were tough enough without being subjected to ridicule for riding a baby bike to school. Nanna—as we all like to call my mother—had become incredibly aware of "image" since her grandchildren were born; or so it seemed to me. I don't recall her being quite so sensitive when it came to image during my junior-high years.

Megan was twelve, and in her short lifespan she had been the proud owner of five bicycles. All purchased with love by her Nanna. Megan had only to grow a titch for Nanna to declare her too big for her bike. In Nanna's eyes Megan had now outgrown the bike bought just two short years earlier, and Nanna deemed it time to buy another bike: a bike worthy of a young girl entering the critical years in junior high, a bike worthy of a young adult. A grown-up bike.

Nanna was a force to contend with when it came to purchasing a new bike. At the bike shop she was terrific; she let Megan pick the style and colour of bike she wanted. It was important to Nanna that Megan like the bike. It was more than just a mode of transportation; it was a statement, an extension of oneself. No cost was too high. (It was lucky for Nanna that Megan hadn't taken to those lightweight racing bikes. Not yet anyway.)

"I like this one, Nanna," stated Megan.

Megan was looking at a mountain bike, painted a glittery metallic blue that changed intensity depending on the light. It was certainly not the most expensive bike in the store, but not the cheapest by any means. It was a nice-looking bike, and that was how Megan was making her choice. Her criteria for judging the merits of a bicycle were based entirely on the bike's appearance. This, of course, is what you expect from most twelve-year-olds; they are going to choose their bikes based entirely on aesthetic appeal. It was important to Megan how the bike looked. Nanna respected that.

"Well, let's take it outside and see how it feels. Get yourself a helmet off that rack and give it a ride," Nanna said.

Nanna knew that no one in their right mind would buy a car without driving it first. Fortunately both Nanna and United Cycle believed the same was true for a bicycle. United Cycle had an outdoor compound accessible only from inside the store. Customers were invited to take the bike of their choice out there to try it out—take it for a spin, one might say.

Nanna beamed as Megan carefully selected her helmet, a requirement for all test drives, and took a little spin around the compound. The bike was a good fit for Megan, just the right size.

"What do you think?" Nanna asked as Megan came to a stop beside her.

That question spun me back in time to when I was entering Grade Seven and getting my first grown-up bike.

*   *   *   *   *

"What do you think, Kelly?" Mom said to me.

"Well, it's okay," I said hesitantly, trying not to show my true feeling, which was one of utter disappointment.

"What do you mean, 'okay'? I thought you wanted this type of ten-speed."

I could see the look of frustration on my mother's face, and I knew what she was thinking. Here she was, on her weekend, taking me to the store to buy a new bike for me, and I appeared to be ungrateful now that we had found what she deemed a great bike for me.

It's not that I didn't want the bike. I did. It's just that the ten-speed my mom had picked out was brown. I didn't want a brown bike; none of my friends would have a brown bike. I wanted a bike that was fire-engine red or sparkling blue or bright yellow. But my mom was so practical, I knew she wouldn't understand.

"I was—well, I was hoping I could get the—that blue bike. It's exactly the same," I stammered in response to my mother, and gave my father a pleading look, a please-help-me-old-guy look.

Both my parents looked over at the blue bike. For all intents and purposes the two bikes were the same, except that one was blue and one was brown. And of course one cost ten dollars more.

"But the blue bike is ten dollars more," my mom said to my dad. "Look at it, Bob. It can't be the same bike."

"It certainly looks like the same bike to me," replied Dad.

"Well, that doesn't make any sense. Go find a clerk to help us," Mom said.

I watched as Dad approached one of the sales staff, a person who had been watching us with a critical eye. I crossed my fingers and prayed as they talked. I prayed that there was enough of a difference in the two bikes to justify the additional ten dollars. My heart skipped a beat when Dad turned and pointed at the beautiful blue bike. I held my breath as he then brought the ugly brown bike to the salesperson's attention. He listened intently to the salesperson for a very short period of time.

Then Dad came walking back toward us.

"It appears as if they are the same bikes," Dad said, and his words broke my heart.

"They can't be," Mom said, showing her surprise.

"Well, they are, according to the salesman," Dad said.

"Well, I don't believe that. That doesn't make any sense at all," Mom said. "If they're the same bikes, how come one costs ten bucks more?"

"The salesman said that nobody wants a brown

bike, so they've dropped the price, hoping to get rid of it," Dad replied.

"Really," Mom said, and I saw a faint smile cross her lips. I knew that smile. That was the trademark smile of Mrs. Let's-Find-A-Deal.

"That's what the man said," Dad replied.

Well, I could have told the clerk and my parents that a brown bike would be slow to move. What teenager—for that matter, what adult—in her right mind would want a brown bike? I certainly didn't need to be told by some clerk in a bicycle store that brown was a less appealing colour for a teenager's bike; I knew that already, and so did every other teenager. It was as clear as the nose on your face. After all, the brown bike was still here in the store, even with a tag that was ten dollars less than the rest of the bikes. It didn't take a team of high-paid marketing executives to figure out that the brown bike was not going to fly out of the store. Apparently, though, the marketing executives had counted on the infamous Mr. and Mrs. Let's-Find-A-Deal. And, luckily for this particular commission salesman, that couple had just walked into this store. My parents were very thrifty people. If there was a deal to be found, it goes without saying that they would find it.

"Well, that's the most ridiculous thing I've ever

heard," Mom said. "And I'm not paying more for a bike just because it's blue, especially not when they're exactly the same bike! In fact, if they want to get rid of that brown bike so badly, I'll bet I can get more than ten dollars off."

At this point in the shopping experience, knowing what was coming, I wanted to disappear into the nearest clothing rack to avoid the humiliation. Push myself way to the back, praying that I'd be completely invisible.

"That's just a scam to charge more for the blue bike," echoed my dad.

"I'd really prefer the blue bike," I interjected.

I was determined to make one final plea for the blue bike. From past experience I knew I would have this bike for a long time, and I wanted to make sure I got something I liked. After all, I was the one who was going to have to ride it onto the school grounds under the critical eyes of my judgmental peers. I really wanted the blue bike.

It was clear, however, that no one was listening to me. Mom and Dad were both at the counter with the salesman, trying to wangle another five dollars off the already reduced brown bike.

I had only ever owned two bikes—my trendy banana-seat bike, which up until that very day I was still riding, and my first two-wheeler, which I had bought with my own money when I was five. My parents had always been money-cautious, and Dad never missed an opportunity to teach me lessons about money, something for which I will be eternally grateful.

My dad was a Fish and Wildlife officer, and when I was five he was stationed in Hinton—campground country. He, of course, knew all the campsites like the back of his hand. He also knew where all the weekend campsite parties were. And so, on the Saturday and Sunday mornings after the big parties, we would hit the campsites, and I would collect the empty bottles. Dad and I were recycling activists long before it was politically correct. My campsite collection drives were quite lucrative. Not only did those bottles buy my first bicycle; they bought me a few savings bonds as well.

At that very moment, as I watched my mom and dad talk to the salesman about the brown bike, I was wishing that we still lived in Hinton: I could have waited for the weekend and picked bottles for the extra fifteen bucks. Unfortunately our bottle-picking days had ended when we moved to Calgary and lost our access to the party campsites.

Mom and Dad went round and round with the salesman for quite a while. Eventually they got the brown bike reduced by fifteen dollars. My humiliation was complete as I wheeled the brown bike out to our vehicle, following my parents who were elated by their latest outstanding deal.

I certainly got my parents' money's worth out of the brown ten-speed. I rode it through junior high, high school, and all through university. Thank goodness I eventually learned to drive and could finally leave the brown bike in my past, or at least in the shed, waiting for a proper burial at the dump. It tugged a little (but only a little) at my heartstrings when, twenty-five years after the purchase of the infamous brown bike, I watched the guys from Junk Removal throw it into the back of the truck and drive off into the sunset on the way to the dump.

*   *   *   *   *

Maybe my parents are more sensitive to the plight of their granddaughters than to that of their daughters, or maybe they just have more money now; I'm not sure. But as we loaded Megan's metallic-blue bike into the back of the van I thought back to my brown ten-speed. I wonder if Megan will ride her metallic-blue bike that long. The way things are going, she might already be riding a new bike when this story is published.

To this day, when I get together with my friends from the good old days, we laugh about lots of things from our past. The one thing someone always brings up is my old brown bike—I hated that bike and everyone knew it. I guess, though, in the big scheme of things, it did serve its purpose. After all, it outlasted several of my dad's cars.

If only it could have been red or blue or yellow. Anything but brown.

No cowboy was ever faster on the
draw than a grandparent pulling
a baby picture out of a wallet.

-Author Unknown

EVERY LITTLE GIRL
SHOULD HAVE ONE

Every little girl should have one was a phrase entirely foreign to me until I had my daughters, and then this expression started to pop up at regular intervals in my conversations with my mother, now known as Nanna.

I remember the first time it found its way into our conversation; my older daughter was about three years old. My husband, Bill, and I were sitting with my mom, my dad, and our two girls on the deck in our backyard one beautiful summer day. My mother was surveying our backyard—assessing it, actually.

"Every little girl should have one," Nanna stated suddenly, out of the blue.

I was confused by her statement. I looked over at her to see who she was talking to and what she was talking about. She wasn't looking at me, or anyone else for that matter; she was just gazing at the backyard and nodding her head as if she were agreeing with someone.

"You have a lot of room in your backyard," Nanna said.

A lot of room, I thought, looking at the thin strip of grass that was all that remained of our backyard. Who was she kidding?

"A lot of room for what?" I asked.

"For a playhouse," she answered.

I didn't think we had a lot of room in our backyard, and certainly not a lot of room for a playhouse. In fact the amount of actual yard that was still available was pretty small. There was barely enough room between the deck and the fence for Bill to turn the lawn mower around when the catch bag was attached.

When we bought the house, the yard had been less than average in size; and then, at Bill's insistence, we had built a huge deck, using up at least two-thirds of the backyard. I had believed the deck was outrageously big when we built it—and my opinion was confirmed when we were able to teach our children to ride their tricycles on the deck surface.

There was very little lawn left in our yard to accommodate a playhouse. And that remaining lawn had a bit of a slope leading down to a gully just before the fence, which made it difficult to use the space for much of anything at all. There was maybe ten feet from the edge of our deck to the fence. Not what I would call a lot of room. But then my mother and I rarely looked at things through the same eyes.

"The space is underutilized, don't you think?" Nanna continued. She was lost in thought, in a world of her own. "I think a playhouse would work very well back here. Yes, every little girl should have a playhouse."

My mind went racing back to my own childhood—after all, hadn't I been a little girl once? Her little girl in fact.

Playhouse. Playhouse. No, it didn't matter how hard I thought, how many repressed childhood memories I tried to conjure up, I could not see a playhouse in my past.

"What do you mean, every little girl should have a playhouse? I never had a playhouse when I was a little girl, Mom," I said.

"Mom?" I repeated, trying to get her attention.

But it was too late; my statement fell on deaf ears. Mom was already down off the deck and was busy checking out the best location for what every little girl needed, a playhouse.

47

"This would be a good spot, here," Nanna said to no one in particular as she surveyed her chosen site.

It didn't take a landscape architect to find the best spot in our yard for a playhouse. I feel relatively confident when I say a playhouse wouldn't have fit anywhere else in the backyard except in the spot she had indicated. And even then, it would be a tight fit.

Nanna bounded back onto the deck and, with a skip in her step, she walked toward the patio doors that led into the kitchen. There she dramatically turned around and looked back toward the spot she had just selected.

"Come here for a second and look, Kelly," she said, beckoning for me to join her at the patio door.

"Look at what?" I asked.

"Just come and look for yourself. You would be able to see the playhouse right here from the patio door," she said. "You could keep your eyes on the girls even if you were in the kitchen."

She paused there as if to reflect on the brilliance of her own plan.

"Pa, how long do you think it would take to build a little playhouse in this backyard?" my mom asked, ignoring me and cleverly luring my dad—Pa, as we lovingly called him—into her plan.

My dad, the incredibly handy man that he is, had been building things for my mother for years.

"We could probably build a simple little playhouse in three or four days, maybe a week," Pa replied. "With the slope in the yard, we would have to dig up a good portion of the lawn, so that we could bury cinder blocks to get a level footing for the floor joists."

"I'll bet we could build it in a weekend if we all pitched in," said Nanna, her eyes alight in anticipation.

Now, if you knew Nanna, you would know that she would not be satisfied with any old playhouse. It had to be a playhouse worthy of the best grandchildren in the world, her grandchildren.

And so the whirlwind began. Nanna got a set of blueprints from a friend who had built a phenomenal playhouse for his children. Pa was sent home to rummage through his workshop—his junk heap, as Nanna liked to call it—for some unused treasure that could be utilized on the playhouse project. Bill was assigned the job of chief earthmover; in this particular case, the only earthmover. He started to dig up the sod and level the cinder blocks to ready the foundation. No one was spared from this project. Nanna assigned jobs to everyone. Never was there a better foreman; "Ramrod Nanna", as we affectionately called her, could boss people around with the best of them.

It didn't take long for me to realize that Bill had drawn the short straw. He was busy toiling away in the blazing sun, beads of sweat standing out on his face as he hauled, set, and levelled the cinder blocks. He anchored them in place with drift pins, then hand-mixed cement and poured it into the cinder blocks to keep them from moving. Pa had picked up some six-inch bolts that he set into the wet cement so that the walls and floor could be bolted to the cinder blocks.

I knew we were in trouble when just the levelling and cementing of the cinder blocks consumed one whole weekend; and so, as had happened with many, many projects that had come before, the playhouse project and Nanna's crew fell a little behind schedule. There were times when I believed the girls would be off to college and the four of us—Bill, Mom, Dad, and I—would still be working on this weekend project.

I should not have been surprised by this, because Pa was famous for underestimating the completion time of a project, and Nanna was just as famous for adding on to a project as it went along. At one point Nanna suggested that we put a loft in the attic, accessible by means of a little rope ladder. It was the only suggestion she made that never saw the light of day. Nanna and Pa working together on a project was a disastrous combination when you were looking for a completion date.

The simple little playhouse was turning into an architectural masterpiece, complete with a cottage door that we split horizontally so that it could be opened from the top or the bottom or both. And the beautifully designed Plexiglas windows that you could slide open and shut were perfect for playing ice cream drive-thru. I fondly remember doing just that on many occasions: In my invisible car I would drive by the Plexiglas window to order from one of my daughters my extra-large mixed cone dipped in chocolate—an invisible, calorie-free cone, the very best kind.

The outside of the playhouse was beautifully finished with tongue-and-groove cedar siding and the crowning glory, cedar shakes. Both were leftovers found in Pa's workshop, treasures from some past projects. Who knows how long that cedar siding had been hanging around. Pa said it was from the early seventies, when Nanna had him build a sauna in our house in Calgary. I know my father well enough to know that those precious cedar boards might have been used for a project before I was even born, and he had been hauling them around for the last four decades, waiting for the perfect opportunity to use them. Nanna and Pa had been living in their current Edmonton home about sixteen years, and I know for a fact that cedar siding was not used for any project in that home. Pa could have been right; knowing his hoarding nature, the siding might have moved with us from Calgary, or our home before that in Hinton.

The cedar siding caused Pa no end of trouble. Now at last he had found a use for it, but unfortunately there was not quite enough to finish the whole playhouse, and it was so old that he had difficulty matching it with something that was available now. Thank goodness Pa was retired. As it was, the cedar siding search added days to our already overshot project schedule, and he ended up travelling to several different stores to get the quantity of siding he needed.

And so it went. The project that was to be accomplished in a weekend, or a week at the most, dragged on throughout the entire summer. Previously planned recreational activities had to be rescheduled or cancelled altogether. Nanna was a tyrant, making all other activities secondary to the completion of the playhouse. My husband forfeited his annual golf game with his high-school buddies. The playhouse was Nanna's priority, and therefore everyone's priority. Nanna made sure it took precedence over everything else.

We discovered that building the perfect playhouse was no small feat. Certainly my mother can be blamed, being the driving force behind the playhouse, but truthfully I must admit that even I got wrapped up in the excitement of the build. I bought a lovely piece of linoleum, laid it myself, then cut the baseboards and hammered them in place.

When the playhouse was finished, Nanna wasn't—she was just beginning. She was gaining momentum and was quickly qualifying for the title of World's Greatest Nanna. She purchased some furniture especially built for a playhouse, a kitchen table and chairs that were just the right size for little bodies. And who could forget the upholstered couch and chair that were custom-made for the "princess palace", a name the playhouse had acquired during the project. People used to tease us that we had a guest house in our backyard. Indeed we did, but you had to be under the age of ten to qualify for residency.

It took more than two months to build it, but I have to admit that, when I saw the finished product there in my backyard, it took my breath away. It was almost nicer than some of the houses on our street. Its beautiful cedar walls and the cedar shakes on the roof glistened from the linseed oil that Bill had patiently massaged into each one of them.

I vividly remember the day Bill oiled those shakes. It must have been 30 degrees Celsius that day as he stood on a ladder in the scorching heat, the sun beating down on him. I can still see the sweat pouring from his brow, and my mom standing there providing "close supervision". She was reminding him that the staining had to be done all at one time to avoid an uneven, two-toned look. Bill really was a good sport; he roasted that day in the heat, but he got the shingles done without any delay, and they glistened in the sun with one even tone.

As I looked at the finished playhouse in all its splendour, I was sure that my girls were the envy of all the little girls on the street. I must admit it was a work of art. From the carefully levelled cinder blocks to the glistening cedar shakes, it was a playhouse to be proud of.

The longer I stared at it, the more I couldn't help but think back to when I was young, before my parents were grandparents and began campaigning for Grandparents of the Year.

*   *   *   *   *

I loved to play house in my backyard when I was a little girl, Nanna and Pa's little girl before they were known as Nanna and Pa. I remember fondly how

I used to drape a sheet over the picnic table in our backyard. That was my playhouse. It didn't have quite as much room as the princess palace they built for my children. You couldn't stand up in my mock playhouse; the ceiling was just too close to the ground. Well, actually, moving around at all was pretty much out of the question—the playhouse was crammed too full with all the stuff I hauled out from the house. Unlike the princess palace, which could remain furnished indefinitely, my picnic palace had to be dismantled each night and all the stuff I had hauled out there taken back inside.

I didn't have any custom-built furniture, but I designed handsome rooms from nothing but pillows, towels, and boxes. I didn't have a split cottage door or Plexiglas windows for playing drive-thru, but I did make a mean mud pie from scratch, right out of the flower garden. My playhouse wasn't much good at keeping you dry from the rain; in fact, the entire house and furnishings were made with such absorbent materials that playing in the rain was not really an option. And some nights I did have to dismantle early because we needed the picnic table to eat outside. But all in all I liked my makeshift playhouse.

When I was young, I had nothing to compare it to; no one I knew had a real playhouse back then.

55

A grandmother is a mother
who has a second chance.

-Author Unknown

THE SACRED RULE

"I have to go to the bathroom," said one of my friends, jumping off my bed and manoeuvering her way toward the door through the Barbie empire we had created on the floor.

Two of my friends and I had dragged everything we could imagine into my bedroom to create the Barbie empire. The hallway from the linen closet to my bedroom was strewn with towels, face cloths, and pillowcases that we had discarded as being not quite the right fit for the Barbie empire. We had chosen every hand towel, face cloth, and pillowcase for its specific colour and texture; they were to be tucked neatly around selected books from my dad's bookshelf. We made all our furniture—beds, couches, and assorted tables—from the books. We painstakingly chose each book for a specific purpose, requiring each to be just the right shape, size, and thickness.

Mom's Tupperware was carefully laid out on the floor to create bathtubs, sinks, and toilets. The upper crust of the Barbie empire even had Tupperware hot tubs in their backyards.

Dishcloths and sewing scraps had been used to design carpets and couches, pillows and chairs. There was not a square inch of floor space that had not been claimed by one Barbie family or the other.

Sometimes my friends and I would get so engrossed in our efforts to set up a vast Barbie empire that we didn't even get a chance to play Barbies. All our time was consumed with the creation of the Barbie empire, working exclusively with stuff we could find around the house.

"I have to go too," said my second friend as she also jumped off the bed and strategically weaved her way across the bedroom floor in an attempt to get to the bedroom door and into the hallway.

Both of my friends had come over to play after school. That was my favourite thing about school, having friends over at the end of a day of hard work and learning. I was lucky I lived so close to the school—my friends could walk home with me any day

I wanted, and we could play or watch television until my mom came home from work.

"Too late!" my first friend screamed as she ran down the hall and into the bathroom, slamming and locking the door behind her.

"Don't you guys have another bathroom?" my second friend inquired.

Of course we have another bathroom, I thought to myself. Or at least we have half of another bathroom. That's what my mom called it: a "half bath". She always said our house had a "bath-and-a-half". I think it was because the second bathroom was really small.

"Well, yeah, we do, but it's in my mom and dad's bedroom," I said.

"Can't I use that one? I really have to go!" my friend pleaded as she crossed her legs to emphasize her need to use the bathroom.

What part of what I just said didn't she understand? I thought.

"No. No, you can't. It's in my mom and dad's bedroom," I repeated. "No one is allowed to go into my mom and dad's bedroom, including the bathroom."

"So? There's nobody home. I'll just go into their room and use the bathroom. No one will know," she said, rolling her eyes at me.

Who was she kidding, no one would know? She was

talking about my mom and dad's bedroom. Maybe she didn't remember meeting my mom and dad. They knew everything. Nobody went into my mom and dad's bedroom, except of course my mom and dad. This was a sacred, never-spoken-of rule.

I don't remember ever being told not to go into Mom and Dad's bedroom; it was something we were born knowing in our family. Mom and Dad probably made the rule when I was in the womb. Dad probably talked to Mom's belly when she was pregnant, first with me and then with my sister, repeating the rule so we would be born knowing that we don't go into their bedroom.

Suddenly I had a clear picture in my head of how Dad had delivered the message: "Do not enter the parents' bedroom; the big bedroom with the big bed is off limits to all children; this is not a negotiable rule," my dad would repeat to my mom's belly over and over again. Yes, that was definitely how it was done.

I suppose if you were dying in the night—you know, you wake up and there's blood gushing from your head—you might be able to go in and roust them out of their sleep. Or if you woke up and the house was on fire—you could smell smoke and see the flames licking at the walls in the living room—it would be okay to wake them and let them know they should get out of the house. But since I had never woken up with blood gushing from my head or smelling our house burning, I had never actually tested those theories, so I'm only guessing that the rule could be broken under those circumstances.

It wasn't so much my mom; it was actually my dad who wanted their room off limits. I know this for a fact because, on the odd occasion when my dad was out of town for work, Mom would sometimes let us, my sister and me, sleep in the big bed with her. The vastness of the king-size bed made for a great adventure—you could stretch right out and never reach the other side. I could roll around, wriggle, and kick, and never touch either my mom or my sister.

"My dad would know," I said.

"Your dad?" she asked.

She gave me a funny look. Sort of like she was questioning what kind of house I came from. She didn't seem to believe me that my dad would know something like that.

I knew that had sounded weird as soon as it came out of my mouth. I tried desperately to save face in the situation.

"I mean, my mom would know," I corrected myself.

"How? How would your mom know?" my friend questioned.

"She just would," I said. "My mom knows stuff. She has a sixth sense about stuff. She can tell sometimes when I've walked on the shag carpet right after she vacuumed and raked it."

"Raked it? Who rakes their carpet?" my friend said, looking at me in disbelief.

I could see I was making the situation worse. With my every comment I was making our family sound more and more like a bunch of eccentrics.

I don't think my friend believed me about raking the carpet. But really, who would make up something like that? I clearly remember watching my mom painstakingly rake her way out of the room. Walking backwards so that all the ridges and gullies would line up perfectly and there would be no visible footprints. To the outside observer it would appear that the rug had been sculpted by an invisible force.

"My mom does, especially if we're having company. She has a special rake for shag rugs, and she always rakes the rug. It makes the carpet look really nice," I said.

"Is there something in their room that you don't want me to see?" my friend asked suspiciously.

I was getting kind of uncomfortable with this conversation. What exactly did that mean—something I didn't want her to see? I had to think about that a little.

What was in there? Just the usual stuff. There was a king-size bed with a white fake-satin bedspread. At the foot of the bed was an oversized afghan that my grandma had had specially made by some old bachelor at the old folks' home in Humboldt, Saskatchewan. I distinctly remember the afghan, because it had a rather pungent smell that never went away even after it had been washed dozens of times.

There was one lone dresser with a very special jewellery box on top. The jewellery box was for my dad's pin collection. I had made that little box for him out of a wooden cigar box and a brand-new velour housecoat my mom had recently bought for me. I remember how upset Mom was when I cut up that housecoat to line the cigar box. However, she did reluctantly agree with me that the lining was what made the box look really nice. It was just the right colour, sort of a shimmery copper. I must admit, though, that the housecoat was kind of ruined after that. After all, who would want to wear a housecoat missing a square foot of cloth in the back?

There were two night tables, one on either side of the bed. Sitting on the night table on Mom's side of the bed was the phone. Mom always answered the phone in the night because my dad got so many work calls in the middle of the night. Sometimes Mom would tell them that my dad wasn't home, so he could get a full night's sleep instead of having to get up long before the break of dawn and go to work. On the night table on Dad's side of the bed was a radio clock. It was a really cool radio clock. It had a long neck on one side with a light on top. You could read with the light, or you could shine it on the big round clock so you could see where the hands were pointing and tell the time. I'm not sure what was in the drawers of the night tables.

Then there was the closet that ran one whole length of the room. I have absolutely no idea what was in there either, but I'm sure that snooping in it would have been punishable by death.

Don't get me wrong—I had been in my parents' room on a few occasions. Once when I had a bad dream and ventured across the hall and woke them up. That was right before they sent me immediately back to my own room. You see, both my parents worked, and they needed their sleep; they didn't have time to deal with bad dreams in the night.

And then there was that one time when my dad had brought home some baby ducks that had to go to the zoo in the morning. They stayed overnight in the bathtub in Mom and Dad's bathroom. I remember, my sister and I were allowed to go into their room then to look at those ducks swimming around in the tub.

At that moment my thoughts were interrupted and I was saved, because my first friend came out of the washroom and my second friend went in. When she came out of the washroom, we weren't talking about my parents' bathroom anymore; we were back in my room, where we continued building the Barbie empire, using my entire bedroom floor.

*   *   *   *   *

Today, years later, when I fondly reflect on how sacred my parents' bedroom was, I have to chuckle to myself at how things change.

Last weekend my daughters Megan and Amy—both toddlers really—had a sleepover at Nanna and Pa's house.

"How was the sleepover?" I inquired after they returned home.

"We made forts and had Kraft Dinner for supper," said Amy with enthusiasm. Her enthusiasm was so unbridled that I felt a pang of guilt. Was she implying that we never build forts or have Kraft Dinner at home?

"We got to eat Kraft Dinner in the fort," Megan chimed in.

"In the fort?" I questioned, just a little taken aback.

"Yes, the fort we built in the living room," Megan said, adding to my surprise.

"Nanna let you eat supper in the living room? On the rug?" I asked.

"Nanna ate in the fort with us," Amy added excitedly.

No wonder Megan and Amy always had such a great time at Nanna and Pa's house. They got to eat in the fort in the living room on Nanna's precious new rug.

WOW. I certainly don't remember that from my childhood. We were never allowed to eat in the living room. We were required to eat at the kitchen table. And we certainly never made a fort in the living room. The forts I recall from my childhood were made out of discarded appliance boxes and generally built in the basement, before it was fully developed. This kept the fort conveniently out of the way, so as not to disrupt the aesthetic appeal of the living room. Once the basement was developed and became part of the formal living area, we were allowed to build our forts only under the basement stairs. I don't ever recall eating in my fort.

Apparently this is why the Kraft Dinner is better at Nanna's than it is at home—because at home we don't get to eat it in the fort or in the living room.

Maybe Nanna's rug was more precious in the 1970s than it is in the twenty-first century.

"So did you get to sleep in the fort too?" I

figured that, since everything else was a go, they must have slept in the fort too.

"No, we slept in the big bed," Amy informed me.

"Wow, the big bed! You mean the big bed in the spare room, right? The queen-size bed in the little bedroom, the room for company," I said, correcting her.

"No, the big bed in Nanna and Pa's bedroom," Amy stated emphatically. She always did know when she was right, even as a small child.

"You mean . . . you both slept with Nanna and Pa in the big bed in their room?" I couldn't believe my ears. Who were they kidding? The Pa I knew would never allow it.

"No, Mom," Amy said, "we didn't sleep with Pa. He slept in the spare room. Just me and Megan and Nanna slept in the big bed."

I knew that now I had heard it all. The Pa I knew never gave up his bed for anyone. This was big! It was like the Berlin Wall coming down all over again. The girls had slept in the big bed—in the sacred room, the room where trespassers were not welcome. My dad, their pa, had slept in the spare room.

What had gone wrong? I wondered. Why had my children been born not knowing the rule, the sacred rule? And then it occurred to me—of course they didn't know the rule, because my dad, their pa, had not spent countless hours repeating the rule to my pregnant belly. And so the rule had been lost, and now the unravelling would begin. First one rule would disappear, then two rules, and soon there would be no rules left.

There would be chaos. Those two little girls would take over Nanna and Pa's home. The grandchildren would get whatever they wanted whenever they wanted it. It would be anarchy. The children, my children, would run wild in my parents' home. My girls would want to go there all the time to revel in the freedom. The girls would like the grandparents, the Nanna and the Pa, better than the Mom and Dad.

And there it was. At last it was clear to me. For the first time I understood their plan, the grandparents' plan. They wanted the grandchildren to like them, to really like them, to like them better than they liked anyone else. It was an ingenious plan, and apparently it was working.

It will be years before I can settle the score, as they say. I will need many things—cunning, ingenuity, a ruthless desire to succeed—but most importantly, I will need to be a grandparent.

ADULTS ONLY

As was the case in many middle-class families in the seventies, our annual family vacation tended to be visits to various relatives. How exotic your vacation destination was depended mainly on where members of your extended family lived.

The large portion of my mom's family lived in Saskatchewan, and so it was without discussion that we headed back to Saskatchewan every summer for our one-week family vacation. Mom's parents lived in the small town of Humboldt, close to the family farm that was then inhabited by her brother and his family. Every year we made the journey—460 long, flat miles—to the place that my mom called home.

The vacations to Saskatchewan were always pretty much the same. They would begin and end with me sprawled in the back seat of a car—a Pontiac Parisienne with a huge back seat, a Ford Meteor with an even bigger back seat, or a Ford Thunderbird with not quite so big a back seat. The make of the car was not important, because my vegetative state was the same all the way to Saskatchewan no matter what car we owned at the time. The high points of my trip occurred whenever I raised my head, looked out across the treeless horizon, and asked hopefully, "Are we there yet?"

Finally we would arrive at our primary destination in Saskatchewan, my grandparents' house. Grandma and Grandpa were always ready for us. There would be four chairs around the kitchen table, with two decks of cards and a notepad and pencil carefully placed at one end. It seemed to me that Grandpa was dealing the cards before we were even through the door, and immediately a game of bridge would begin.

Bridge was a favourite card game of my grandparents; a card game requiring only four people, children not included. Now, I knew how to play bridge—Mom and Dad had taught me—but I was never invited into their all-adult game. At first I would loiter around the kitchen table, hoping that someone would need to go to the bathroom and I would get the opportunity to play a hand or two. However, all four adults seemed to be able to time their bathroom visits for when they were the dummy hand, laying their cards down for their partner to play.

As hope faded for a chance to edge my way into the game, I would begin begging my mom and dad to take me to the farm, where my cousins lived. But no one in my family walks away from a game of bridge, good or bad. If they're on the way to a quick rubber, they don't want to stop because they can smell victory; and if they're losing at the moment, they don't want to quit because they know it takes only one good hand and they'll be right back in it. There is no greater joy in bridge than cutting off the leg of an opponent who is on the way to a quick rubber.

Eventually I would get tired of standing around the table waiting to get a nod into the game, and I would wander down the hall to the spare room, where my grandmother kept her sewing and crafts.

My grandmother was a wonder with all sorts of crafts. There was not much waste in her way of doing things, and she could reuse anything. She saved every scrap of material from every piece of clothing she could get her hands on, and she made those scraps into something useful: a blanket, a pillow, a rug, or a Christmas ornament. I would wile away considerable time sorting through my grandmother's latest crafts and her scrap material.

The clatter of dishes in the kitchen was my call to action. The card players always stopped for food; after all, bridge was important, but not so important that a person should miss a meal for it. Now, if my timing was right, I could get my ride to the farm. It was imperative that I approach my dad during the preparation of the meal, because once the banquet began, the window of opportunity would close. So it was during the food preparations that Dad would drive me out to the farm, where I would spend the remainder of my family vacation, occasionally seeing my parents but mostly hanging out with my aunt and my cousins.

Looking back, I wonder how my aunt ever survived summers. Summer was always a very busy time on the farm, and she had to deal with a multitude of tasks. Probably the most demanding, certainly the most important, of her responsibilities was catering to the men working in the fields. Preparing enough food for them—whether they ate it in the kitchen or she took it to them in the field—was job one. But on top of that she had to deal with the steady stream of relatives (my mom had eight brothers and sisters), a barrage of road-weary, hungry relatives who, like my family, came home for the annual summer visit. I'm sure it wasn't just my imagination; they really did show up, eat, and then abandon their children at the farm before heading back to town to visit and play cards with my grandma and grandpa. Just like my parents did.

I liked the farm. It was a curiosity to me, a city kid. The farm was nothing like the city. On the farm I felt free. And I was free—free to roam and find adventure. There was no curfew on the farm. It seemed to me we could have played hide-and-seek all night in the trees surrounding the house on the farm, and that would have been all right.

My cousins and I were always building forts and tree houses. We never seemed to complete any of our projects, but nobody cared. We could abandon a partially finished structure; just walk away. We didn't even clean up when we were done.

One summer we found a lot of dead birds, baby birds or at least parts of them, and we started a graveyard. We would have services for the birds, taking turns being the priest and the grieving family. When we tired of the graveyard, we turned our attention to the dozens of wild kittens around the farm. We would play with them for hours, dressing them up and pretending they were our babies. The kittens were fun to play with and we had no responsibility to care for them. The life of a kitten on the farm seemed to have little value; it was so different from the way a house cat in the city was treated. But then, farm kittens never lived in the house.

As much as I liked the farm, I was a little bit afraid of it too. For one thing, the sheer size of the buildings and the equipment was intimidating. I knew the equipment was important, because it was well cared for and we were never allowed to play with it, but I never did understand what everything was used for.

My number one fear at the farm, though, was the dugout. It was a fear that my mother had beaten into me. The dugout meant danger.

"Kids drown all the time in dugouts," my mom would say whenever the subject of the farm came up. "Don't go near the dugout."

And then someone would tell a frightful story of a young farm girl or boy who had drowned in a dugout. It is entirely possible that the story was always about the same child, but during those years I thought the neighbouring dugouts had swallowed up dozens of kids.

Dugouts were to be avoided at all costs. As a child I never understood the purpose of a dugout; no one ever told me and it never occurred to me to ask. On many occasions while I was being reminded of the dangers of a dugout, I would think to myself, Why don't they just get rid of the dugout? I pictured a dugout as a pit of quicksand with a pool of water on the surface. Unsuspecting kids—kids who were not smart enough to fear the dugout like I did—would get sucked into the dugout, never to be seen again. I was smart; I avoided the dugout.

Consequently it was years before I even saw a real dugout, and it wasn't at my cousins' farm. In all the years I vacationed there I never saw that dugout, and to this day I don't even know where it is on the farm. Dugouts were one of my first experiences with a fear of the unknown.

I was also frightened of the granaries, although that fear had nothing to do with my mother. My older cousin had a great time one summer holding me upside down by the ankles over the chute on the side of the granary, threatening to drop me in. He told me that, if he dropped me into the granary, I would drown in the wheat. He said it wouldn't help if I struggled to get out; the more I struggled, the faster I would sink into the wheat and suffocate. I was scared to death while he was enjoying himself. He laughed and laughed as I dangled, screaming and flailing, upside down over that opening.

That was a life-altering experience for me. For many years afterward I had horrendous dreams of being thrown into the granary. In my dreams, even though I knew I wasn't supposed to, I would always struggle to get out—I couldn't help myself. People would crowd around the chute trying to save me, but I would be sinking farther and farther into the wheat. Then, just as a hand touched mine, before I could be rescued—I would wake up. I blame my claustrophobia on that childhood experience in the granary. Whether or not that is true, I take some comfort in holding my cousin responsible for my irrational fear of closed-in places.

The annual trek back to Saskatchewan exposed me to many things that I would never otherwise have experienced.

The indescribable stench of my cousin's pig barns, for example. As soon as I stepped through the barn door, the acrid smell took my breath away. My throat seized up and I couldn't breathe. I would be led back outside, gasping for fresh air. Actually craving the fresh air of the city, because nothing in the city ever smelled that bad—at least, not in my limited, suburban experience.

The farm was the first place I drove a motor vehicle: driving through the farm fields with reckless abandon—but no licence. I had my mother's permission, of course, but my dad had a fit when he found out I had driven the Thunderbird wildly through the back fields. He gave me a blistering lecture on safety, and how lucky I was not to have ripped off the oil pan.

And I'll never forget my first beer, at age twelve, out in the middle of a field with my cousins and a bunch of local teenagers, all farm kids. As the years passed, I came to know that farm kids never had any trouble coming up with beer—no matter how young they were.

All things considered, the farm was a satisfying vacation for a child in the seventies. I had fun year after year after year—but then, I had nothing to compare it with.

Both of my parents worked full-time in the seventies, and our vacations were limited by the amount of vacation time that their jobs allowed them. But two weeks of that time was always set aside for their adult-only winter vacation. Mom and Dad always took a winter holiday to some warm, exotic destination. In the early years it was usually Mexico or Hawaii; in later years they started to choose more adventurous destinations, places like Africa, Australia, or Costa Rica.

It never occurred to me that I should go along on those adult-only winter vacations. Winter holidays to warm climates were for the mom and dad in a family. Summer holidays to visit the relatives were for the family. I grew up believing that was the way it was. I accepted that; it was my lot in life.

Years later, now that I am an adult myself, I am part of a new scenario, a new experience, one that contradicts the lessons of my youth.

*   *   *   *   *

As I sit on a plane at the start of my summer vacation, I am struck by the oddity of this trip. We are heading out for a family vacation in a warm climate. I'm sitting with my husband; my two small children, both under the age of five; and let's not forget the king and queen of adult-only vacations, my mom and dad. The six of us are on our way to California to stay at the Lawrence Welk resort. This is only seven short months after the six of us have returned from our warm winter holiday in Ixtapa, Mexico. I don't fully understand how this turn of events came to be. My inner child points out that we should be heading to Saskatchewan to visit relatives.

When we arrive at the Lawrence Welk resort, there are things that remind me of my summer trips to Saskatchewan, but somehow they're never quite parallel. My dad, who always had to be pestered to drive me to the farm, is very concerned that his granddaughters get to where they want to be, and he immediately takes them to one of the resort pools for a swim. He doesn't drop them off at the pool and come back to the room to play some cards, though. No, he stays at the pool with them, swimming in the deep end with both girls riding on his back.

Don't get me wrong—my dad will eventually return to the room with the girls, where we will finally get to play some cards. But not the bridge or canasta that I would prefer; instead, we'll play old maid and crazy eights so that the girls can be included. It wouldn't be fair if they were excluded and felt left out.

Unfortunately, however, Megan and Amy won't get the opportunities I had on my summer vacations. They won't get to visit a pig barn on a real farm and experience pigs in all their putrid glory. On the farm (of sorts) that they will get to visit—the Wild Animal Park in San Diego—they will go into an enclosure with rainbow lorikeets flitting about. The birds will land on the girls' heads, and hop nimbly to drink nectar from the containers they hold in their hands.

And no, the girls won't get to drive a Thunderbird through a farmer's field without a licence—but they will get to drive a scaled-down Porsche at Disneyland's Autopia.

Yes, it seems that my mother in all her grandparenting wisdom doesn't believe in adult-only vacations anymore—at least not for me, her adult daughter. Since the birth of her grandchildren, all her winter holidays have been open to everyone; in fact she encourages her grandchildren to take part in all her holidays. "The more the merrier" is her new philosophy.

I wish my mother had adopted that philosophy when I was young; I would have been more than happy to have her drag me off to a warm exotic climate every winter.

If your baby is "beautiful and perfect, never cries or fusses, sleeps on schedule and burps on demand, an angel all the time" you're the grandma.

-Teresa Bloomingdale

THE JACKET

"This closet is a mess!" I said, and I could feel my temperature rising. "Where did all this stuff come from?"

I was disgusted by the state of the front closet. I was simply trying to hang up one jacket, but I was unable to find an unused hanger anywhere in the closet. Not that it mattered. I could tell from looking at the compacted outerwear that I would never find even a sliver of space to cram in one little girl's jacket.

It wasn't that our front closet was small. It was a good size; huge, in fact, because we had deliberately designed it that way when we built the house. I swore that in this new house I wouldn't run

84

short of closet space as we had in our previous house—I had suffered with small closets in all the houses I had lived in, but not anymore.

When we first moved into the house, my newest hall closet had seemed cavernous. That closet had almost too much room, if I dare say so. There was plenty of space left even after we had moved our outerwear in. But the longer we lived in the house, the less space we seemed to have. Only three short years later, either we were collecting too much stuff, or the closet was getting smaller.

In my fit of anger I started yanking the jackets from the closet and tossing them in a heap on the living-room floor.

"What are you doing?" asked my husband as he stared at the growing heap of clothing. "Have you lost your mind?"

"We have to get rid of some of these jackets! And did you see how many shoes are stacked in there on the floor? We can't possibly be using all this stuff," I said. "Where did it all come from?"

My flurry of closet-cleaning slowed a little as I came to jackets that represented various stages of the girls' lives. I paused momentarily at each jacket that marked the passing of time and quietly reflected on how quickly my children were growing up. There was the fuzzy pink coat that Nanna had bought for Megan when she was just learning to walk. I loved that little coat; and I apparently hadn't come to terms with parting with it, as Megan was now eleven and I still had it in my front closet.

There was the Mickey Mouse rain jacket with matching umbrella that Nanna had bought for Amy about five years prior to this closet-cleaning frenzy. Adorable, but the jacket had never been worn, as was apparent from the price tags still dangling from the collar.

There was the winter coat that I had bought for Amy last October, and Megan's coat from last year that I was waiting for Amy to grow into. There was the winter coat that Megan was wearing now—a gift from her Nanna—and the ski jacket her Nanna had bought her because she thought that the other winter coat would not be warm enough on the ski slopes.

There were the matching vests that Nanna had got the girls for days when it was too warm for the winter jacket but not warm enough for their heavy sweaters—also hanging in the closet.

There were the two fake-sheepskin jackets: "I got them on sale! They'll be perfect for the fall," Nanna had said that early spring day when she had proudly burst into our house and given them to the girls.

And then, of course, there was the assortment of jackets Bill and I had accumulated. Winter, fall, and spring jackets. Heck, I still had both our high-school jackets in that closet. Not that there was even a remote possibility that either of us would ever fit into those sentimental keepsakes again.

It took me a couple of hours to go through the jackets and sort the keepers from the ones that had to go. Tedious as it was, however, this actually turned out to be paid work—I went through all the pockets from the get-rid-of pile, and I was excited to find a whopping twenty dollars and change. When I finished, three green garbage bags full of jackets and one full of shoes sat ready to take to Goodwill. I had removed nearly half of the clothing from the closet.

It seemed like only days later that Nanna showed up carrying a shopping bag from Thrifty's, one of the girls' favourite clothing stores.

Nanna has always been very fashion-conscious, keeping her finger on the pulse of the fashion industry. She spends a great deal of time and money ensuring that her own closet is always full of the latest trends. She has tried for years to lure me into the world of the fashion-conscious, with little success. Much to Nanna's disappointment, I am a comfort person; "low-maintenance" is how I like to refer to myself. I choose my clothes by how they feel and their functionality for any given task. I don't care if my sweater is ten years old and out of style. I crave comfort, so as long as that sweater is comfortable and keeps me warm when I walk in the wind, I'm happy.

After Megan and Amy were born, Nanna saw new hope for the state of fashion in her family. I think she secretly believed that the girls would make up for my complete lack of concern or interest in supporting the fashion industry. She immediately began dressing my children in the latest fashion for babies, then toddlers, then children, then tweens, and now teenagers. Nanna loved to shop for the latest fashions, all the while looking for a deal. She had done a great job over the years keeping the girls in style and their closets filled to bursting with an ample supply of everything they needed, and more; and of course it was always the latest style.

Thrifty's is a store that appeals to the young crowd; and so I knew as soon as Nanna set the bag on the counter in my kitchen that it contained something for the girls. And I was right. It contained five T-shirts that we could add to Amy's already bulging bedroom closet and, even though it was April, a new winter jacket.

"I know Amy doesn't need another jacket, but the

sale was so good I just couldn't pass it by," Mom said as she carried the jacket out to the front closet.

Without any trouble she picked out one of the many unused hangers and hung Amy's new jacket in the front closet. It was then that she stopped and carefully inspected the closet. She walked from one end to the other, pausing wherever a large space presented itself. It was eerie, almost as if she were measuring the empty spaces for more jackets.

"Your closet is nearly empty," she said.

An empty closet is like an invitation to a person who loves to shop, especially a shopaholic Nanna.

$$* \quad * \quad * \quad * \quad *$$

Late one sweltering summer afternoon when I was eleven, I returned home from a day at the lake, where I had enjoyed a refreshing swim with my friend. Our house was alive with excitement. Apparently Mom and Dad had gotten a great deal at some store that was closing out. My sister was strutting around as proud as a peacock, sporting a brand-new baby-blue eiderdown jacket, even though it was unbearably hot in the house. It was a really puffy jacket, complete with a puffy eiderdown hood that snapped onto the back of the collar. My sister looked like a baby-blue Michelin man, the jacket was so puffy. Or better yet, she looked as if she had been eaten alive by a baby-blue Michelin man, because the jacket was a little too big and her face almost disappeared inside the puffy baby-blue eiderdown hood. But that didn't seem to bother her, as she continued to strut around the house in her jacket, beads of sweat forming all over her face. I could only imagine how she must be sweating on the inside of the jacket.

"Kelly, you won't believe the deal we found today!" shouted my mom from the kitchen.

"Yeah, I can see Robin's jacket," I replied.

Sometimes I was glad when the great deals didn't include me. I could definitely live without the baby-blue-Michelin-man eiderdown look.

"That's not the half of it," she said as she raced around the corner from the kitchen wearing the exact same jacket as my sister, right down to the baby-blue colour.

Oh lord, it gets worse, I thought. Now I was actually feeling bad for my sister, who obviously didn't realize how not-cool it was to be strutting around in the same jacket as her mother.

"Wow, that's really something," I said. "Lucky for you, and . . . and for Robin. . . . Matching jackets." Poor Robin, I thought.

"Can you believe the store had these on sale for fifty percent off the last sale price," she said. "We got these jackets for practically nothing!"

My mom could barely contain herself, she was so excited.

It was then that my dad joined us from the kitchen.

"They are one hundred percent eiderdown," my dad said.

He was also sporting a brand-new eiderdown jacket and, except for the fact that his was navy blue, it was exactly the same as the ones my mom and sister were wearing.

"You could wear these jackets in an Arctic blizzard and stay nice and toasty warm," he said.

"But we don't live in the Arctic, Dad," I said. "We live in Calgary, and it's really not that cold here in the winter."

"Never have to worry about the coldest day in Calgary either," he said, and he chuckled. "Not in this jacket. Best closing-out sale we've been to in a long time."

The direction this fashion show was taking was making me just a mite uncomfortable. For, in the Adams family, where there are three great deals on eiderdown jackets, you just know there are going to be four.

"Robin, go get Kelly the surprise we got for her," my mom said to my sister.

Robin ran into the kitchen and came back with,

you guessed it, none other than the third baby-blue eiderdown jacket.

"You're kidding," I said, not trying to hide my disappointment. "For me?"

It was a rhetorical question, really. I knew, and so did everyone else, that of course the jacket was for me. Unless I could come up with some long-lost sibling, there was no one else it could possibly be for. I reluctantly took the jacket from my sister.

"Gee, thanks, " I said.

"Go ahead, try it on!" my mom said excitedly.

"Now?" I asked. "But it's so hot in here. I'm sweating just thinking about it."

"C'mon, don't be a spoilsport. We want to see how it looks. Everyone else has theirs on," she said.

I reluctantly put my left arm into the armhole, but my hand never pushed all the way through to the hole at the end of the sleeve. I put my right arm into the right armhole, and again my arm was too short and my hand never pushed through to the opening. I stood helplessly as my mom zipped up the jacket and pulled the hood up over my head, tying the string up snug around my face. The jacket hung to just above my knees. I knew without looking in the mirror that I rivalled my sister now for the baby-blue-Michelin-man look-alike. I stood there for a moment, unable to say anything, before I too broke out into a sweat.

Mom walked all around me, sizing up the jacket.

"Perfect," she said when she had thoroughly inspected me from every angle.

"I-I think it's too big," I stammered.

"No, no, it's just right. We bought it like that on purpose. It will fit you in the winter," my mom said. "You might have to roll up the sleeves a bit for the first winter, but by next winter it will fit great."

And sure enough, she was almost right. In fact, it fit me for quite a few winters—four in all, if I remember correctly. By the fourth winter the jacket was a perfect fit. My hands finally found the holes at the end of the sleeves. Although eventually I grew into the jacket, I never did warm up to the style.

Back in the seventies I had only one winter jacket at a time, and for the second half of the decade it was a baby-blue eiderdown. I didn't get a new jacket every winter, every spring, and every fall just because the styles changed. In the Adams household you got a new jacket only when you outgrew the one you were currently wearing.

In my younger days, when my whole family ventured out in wintertime, people didn't have any trouble recognizing us—we were the happy family of four with the matching jackets. The old guy in the dark-blue jacket was my dad, in case anyone might confuse us by age or gender.

It was lucky for Mom and Dad that the baby-blue eiderdown jacket fit me for a long time, because in all the years I lived at home they never found another closing-out sale like that one. Ask anyone in my family and they will tell you it's true—great sales like that one don't come along every day.

What children need most are
the essentials that grandparents
provide in abundance. They give
unconditional love, kindness, patience,
humour, comfort, lessons in life.
And most importantly cookies.

-Rudolph Guiliani

A DOG'S LIFE

An eerie silence greeted us as we entered the house after school. Our arms were heaped with the typical after-school gear—knapsacks, lunch kits, snow pants. In her usual fashion Amy dropped her armload in the entrance and raced to open the door to the laundry room, excited to reunite with her dogs after a long day at school.

"Hey, buddies, how was your day?" she asked as she swung open the door. She stopped short as she peered into the room. "Where are the dogs?"

I too peered into the laundry room expecting to see the dogs. They should have bounded from the room to greet us—wagging their tails, yelping happily, jumping up on us, and generally expressing their joy at our return. Their absence explained the silence that had greeted us.

"They're probably at Nanna's house," I replied.

I don't know why I was surprised. For the past few weeks the dogs had rarely been home when we returned from school. The kids kept asking the same question day after day after day because the dogs continued to be gone day after day after day when we returned home. I started to feel like a stuck record.

"Where are the dogs, Mom?"—"They might be at Nanna's house."

"The dogs aren't in the laundry room. Where are they?"—"They must be at Nanna's house."

"I can't find the dogs, where are the dogs?"—"At Nanna's house."

Before we get any further into this story, let me make it clear that these are not Nanna's dogs. We do not share ownership of these dogs. They were not at one time Nanna's dogs. We are not caring for these dogs because of some residential ruling that bans dogs from Nanna's home. They are our dogs.

It all began after we moved into our new house in Edmonton, just a stone's throw from Nanna and Pa's house. Nanna quickly developed a new addition to her daily routine; I'm guessing it started the first morning the girls went to school. She began picking up our two toy poodles, Spunky and Patch, immediately after the kids had gone to school and I had left for work. Picking up our dogs seemed to be her number one priority, even ranking ahead of her much-savoured morning coffee.

"Mom, why do you need to take the dogs every day when we're not home?" I asked her shortly after I realized that this activity was in danger of becoming a daily event, if it wasn't already.

"I don't mind taking the dogs," she said, evading my question.

"I know, but why do you take them every day?" I asked again.

"I think those little dogs need to go for a walk, and I walk every day," she said. "I like to take them along. It's good exercise for them, and I enjoy their company."

There it was—very simple—Nanna felt the dogs needed to be walked every day. And since no one at our house was doing it, she was more than happy to take on the job. How could you argue with that logic? The dogs and my mother got their exercise and also kept each other company.

Now, it is true, and I am embarrassed to admit, that we rarely walked our dogs. I could make a million excuses for this.

I could tell you that we were so busy with the kids' after-school activities that we just didn't have the time to get the dogs out every day—or most days, for that matter.

I could argue that we didn't want the girls to take the dogs out on their own because the girls were too young to venture out onto the city streets without adult supervision. Of course, I could have gone with the girls, but after I got home from work, made supper, tidied up, threw in a load of laundry, and made lunches for the next day, there was just no time left in the evening to walk the dogs. (Well, I didn't actually make lunches for the next day; that was Bill's job.)

Another excuse—and this one is my favourite—is that, since the dogs were so little, we could exercise them in the house just by throwing the ball around in the kitchen or up and down the stairs. The dogs would chase the ball anywhere, and it gave them plenty of exercise for their size.

Actually, Amy loved to throw the ball or the stuffed bone or the rawhide chewable, and the dogs loved to race after it and bring it back.

"Look at me, Mom," Amy would say. "I'm training my dog. I'm going to be a dog trainer when I grow up."

My guilt over not exercising our dogs allowed me

to buy into the dog-walking story for a while, but I wasn't convinced that the daily walk was Nanna's real reason for taking the dogs, because once she got them to her house she would keep them there for the rest of the day. And I was right to be skeptical: As time wore on, it became apparent that these visits to walk the dogs were about a lot more than that.

Apparently Nanna had decided that leaving the dogs locked in the laundry room all day was cruel to the dogs. It was unfair to confine them to such a small room for hours at a time. She was saving them from negligent owners who selfishly went to work every day, leaving poor Patch and Spunky home alone to fend for themselves in the confines of the laundry room.

It is true that we lock up our dogs when we leave the house. We have made a lovely spot for them in the laundry room. They have two big beds, one for each dog, and plenty of room to walk around and stretch. We feed them in the morning and let them go outside to do their business before we shut them in. We're confident that the dogs are fine until we get home from our day.

We lock both dogs up so they won't get into anything in the house. Our dogs find any kind of food irresistible; opportunity need only present itself. We learned this lesson the hard way. On one occasion we gave them the run of the house, and they showed their appreciation by rummaging through the garbage and strewing it around the house. We were slow learners, because on another occasion the little dears discovered a bucket of Halloween candy on the floor in one of the girls' rooms. When we arrived home, we found bits and pieces of coloured candy wrapper all over the house. We even found a large stash of wrappers behind a chair in the family room—apparently the ceremonial unwrapping site.

Patch and Spunky never seemed to mind the confines of the laundry room. They would curl up on their beds and sleep all day while we were at work. In the evening, when we were home, they would be up and about. They would chase the girls around the house, barking and fetching their ball and the stuffed bones.

After our move into Edmonton and Nanna's unofficial adoption of the dogs, their daytime sleeps became a thing of the past. Now that they were up all day with Nanna, everything changed. They were exhausted from their long walk every day, and they began to sleep all evening when we were home. Not even a running child or a thrown ball could motivate them. On a good night Patch could sometimes be enticed to walk a few steps and retrieve a ball, but

Spunky would only lift her head from the arm of the chair, look around, and yawn before closing her eyes and going back to sleep. Both dogs were saving their energy for another exhausting day with Nanna.

I started to get concerned when Patch quit eating in the morning and began throwing up. We took her to the vet, who assured us there was nothing wrong with the dog. She had not lost any weight and seemed as well as usual. The vet suggested that the vomiting might be a reaction to a new food in her diet. But we had not changed her diet. She had been eating the same dog food for years. We never fed our dogs "people food", as we liked to call it.

One evening, shortly after Nanna had returned the dogs, one of them threw up on the little rug at the back door.

"Yuck, the dog threw up!" exclaimed Amy when she found the vomit. She immediately left the room in disgust.

I went to clean up the latest installment of vomit and discovered something odd.

"Bill, come here and look at this," I called to my husband.

"Look at what?" he asked.

"Come and look at this dog puke," I said.

"I am not looking at the dog puke," he replied, as disgusted as his daughter.

"Seriously, look at this puke. It looks liked chewed-up carrots," I said.

That got his attention. He came over and looked at the dog puke.

"How would the dogs get into carrots?" he asked no one in particular.

"I have absolutely no idea," I said.

"Girls!" he bellowed.

Both girls came running from different directions. Those were the days when they were still young enough to respond to our bellowing. The good old days.

"Did either of you leave carrots where the dogs might get into them?" he asked.

"I didn't leave any carrots anywhere. Honest, Dad!" replied Amy.

"Not me," said Megan.

Bill turned to me. "Were the dogs at your mom's today?"

I was dialling the number before he even finished the sentence.

"Mom," I said into the phone, "did you feed the dogs carrots today?"

"Well, just a few," Mom replied. "They love carrots."

"Have you fed them carrots before?" I asked, already knowing what the answer would be.

103

"Sometimes they have carrots for their treat," she said. "And they really like crackers too."

"Do you feed the dogs every day when they're at your house?" I asked.

"I always give them one treat," she said. "Just one little treat."

"Don't feed the dogs," I said to my Mom.

"Oh," she replied. It was a noncommittal *Oh*. I had heard it many times from my mother over the years. It was the tone that was noncommittal, not so much the *Oh* itself.

"I mean it, Mom. They are throwing up. You're not doing them any favours. They are just getting sick."

Apparently my emphatic plea fell on deaf ears, however, because this particular problem continued for quite some time. The dog usually tried to get outside before she threw up, but on one occasion she was late to react to the throw-up call and vomited on a brand-new wool rug. We loved that rug; it had been expensive, and we knew we would have it for quite some time.

Bill was angry. He called an emergency family meeting on the spot.

"This situation with the dogs cannot continue!" he declared.

No one said a word. We just looked at him. Anger was out of character for him. He was usually a model of the easy-going guy.

"We have to make a decision," Bill went on. "Either the dogs have to go or Nanna has to go."

Amy, in all her innocence (she was only seven at the time), was the first to respond.

"I really want to keep the dogs . . ." she said hesitantly.

"Amy, Dad is just kidding. We can't get rid of Nanna," said Megan.

I could see relief cross Amy's face. Choosing the dogs over Nanna had obviously been a difficult choice for her.

"Talk to your mother," Bill said to me. "This is getting to be ridiculous."

I did talk to my mother. I talked and talked and talked. But as time went on, not much changed with Nanna and the dogs. We started to feel as if the dogs weren't really ours, and I think the dogs started to feel that way too. In fact Patch would sometimes sit by the front door all evening, waiting for her rightful owner—Nanna—to come back and pick her up.

I felt as if I was losing control—control of my dogs, control of my mother. Not that I ever really had control of my mother, which is evident in the telling of this story. I begged that she not take the dogs every day.

"Mom, please, not for the whole day!" I said. "I think the dogs are getting confused as to who they belong to."

Nanna, however, is a free spirit. Nanna does what she wants when she wants to do it. My pleas went unanswered. She continued to take the dogs all day, every day.

Had Nanna given her evil plan any sort of thought, it would have been easy for her to pull the wool over our eyes. She would have figured out that she could take the dogs every day as long as she brought them home before any of us returned from school or work and she didn't feed them any food that they would give back to us later. None of us would have been the wiser. But no; she liked giving the dogs little treats, and she didn't want to risk misjudging when we would be arriving home. The thought of poor Patch and Spunky being in the laundry room for even a short time was more than she could take. Instead, she would keep them for as long as she wanted, until at last our frustration peaked, and we called and asked her to please bring them home. She would rather face our wrath than have those dogs locked up.

The irony in this story is only truly apparent if you look back through time to when I myself was growing up. I was lucky to have a great dog named Fang. Fang was also a poodle; she was black, and she was the toughest toy poodle ever.

I remember vividly one occasion when a gopher showed its face in our yard. Without any concern for her own safety, Fang chased that gopher into a small opening under our front steps. She clawed at the dirt, widening the hole, and raced in behind the gopher. With both the gopher and the dog underneath our front steps, an unseen battle took place. The noise from the struggle—the growling, the snarling, and the squeaking—was unbearable to me, only a child at the time. I remember crying and screaming that my dog was being killed.

Suddenly everything went deathly quiet. I held my breath. Then I watched as, to my relief, my tough toy poodle proudly emerged from under the steps with a dead gopher set firmly between her teeth.

Even as a child I knew it was important for dogs to get their exercise. But we never walked our dog, none of us—not me, not my mom, and not my dad. Oh, our dog still got plenty of exposure to the outdoors all right. In fact, not a day went by that Fang didn't feel the wind through her fur. Every day, without fail, one of us opened our front door and let our little toy poodle run free.

Fang was a smart dog. It never mattered how long

you let her roam; Fang always found her way back home. Fang could be out of the house for a whole day, and we would only have to stand on our front steps and bellow her name at the top of our lungs. She would eventually come charging down the road, heading for home.

I know what you're thinking—pretty good for a little toy poodle out in the country, wandering alone all day and always finding her way home. Except that we didn't live in the country. No sir, we lived smack in the middle of a Calgary suburb. Fang was an urban roamer. How that dog managed to live to a ripe old age is beyond my comprehension when I reflect on the traffic she must have encountered on her daily journeys. The fact that she was able to avoid the clutches of the infamous local dog catcher for all those years is a true testament to her intelligence.

And I know why Fang was so quick to run for freedom when that front door opened. Simply put, she was locked up all day in the basement workroom while the rest of the family were all at school and at work for the day.

Grandparents are there to help the child get into the mischief they haven't thought of yet.

-Gene Perret

CHILDHOOD SCARS

We looked as if we were a small caravan of nomads, travelling with all our worldly possessions, children in tow. As we entered the water park, you could barely distinguish that there was a family under the mountains of equipment we were carrying for our afternoon outing: towels, coolers, drinks and snacks, flotation devices, goggles, snorkels, water noodles, children—

Well, we weren't exactly carrying the children. The children were running ahead, bursting with energy at the thought of a day at the water park. I, their mother, on the other hand, was exhausted; and the adventure had only begun. It wasn't so much that I was exhausted from the journey as from my growing anxiety. Anxiety feels a lot like exhaustion, and my anxiety was rising the closer I came to the pool.

Public pools began to give me the creeps as a teenager, and the feeling had only intensified as I became an adult. I could never shake the thought of pee, vomit, and bacteria. I became anxious every time we ventured out to a public pool. By the time I had readied the entire family for the outing, I was a big ball of anxiety, in need of a rest. I envied the people who were unaware of—or who could block out the thought of—all the germs and who-knows-what that lurk at a pool facility.

"Don't run, girls—" I started to say, but it was too late. Amy had fallen and scraped her knee on the rough flooring of the pool deck. I hurried to her side, kneeling down beside her.

"Looks like you've got a little scrape there," I said, trying not to make a big deal of it.

"It really hurts, Mommy," she said, big tears welling up in her eyes.

"You'll be fine, let's just . . ."

My words of tenderness were lost as, out of the corner of my eye, I saw something scurry across the floor and into a bed of foliage.

"Do we have cockroaches in Alberta?" I asked my husband, completely forgetting Amy's injury.

"No," he stated emphatically, giving me a funny look.

"I know we don't have them in our house," I countered, so as not to look like a complete dim-wit. "I mean, could they live here, in Alberta, in the water park, amidst the greenery, with all this humidity? 'Cause I'm sure I just saw a little tiny cockroach run into those plants over there."

Cockroaches give me the creeps. Maybe it's because I'm exposed to them so rarely, or maybe it's because they're insufferable creatures that will outlast mankind. But just the thought of cockroaches is enough to make my skin crawl. Now, I am certainly not a leading authority on the cockroach; in fact, I have only briefly encountered them while vacationing. In Mexico I've seen cockroaches that are at least three inches long. Maybe even longer—I've never actually taken the time to accurately measure them. I'm always too busy screaming "Cockroach!" and propelling myself in the opposite direction.

The blur that scurried across the floor at the water park was certainly not three inches long, probably closer to half an inch, but *cockroach* had been the first thing that came to mind. I was pretty sure that I wouldn't be able to get my mind off the alleged cockroach sighting for the entire day we would be at the water park.

As I was saying, I had already developed a distaste for community pools. After my brief involvement with competitive swimming at a very young age, I lost interest in the whole public-swimming concept.

Even as a teenager, whenever I was in a pool, I found myself thinking about all the people who might have relieved themselves in the water that I was swimming in. I knew without a doubt that little kids who were having heaps of fun in the pool were not going to get out of the water and make their way to the nearest washroom if they only had to pee. No way would kids in the heat of fun do that. After all, who would know, and who could tell? They would simply pause, move away from other swimmers, look around, smile, and—without a second thought—pee in the pool. I know this for a fact, because as a young child I peed in the pool a few times myself.

Then there was the fateful family trip to California, filled with hours of fun in the sun and, of course, in the outdoor swimming pool. Everything was going well, and in the excitement of the event I had managed to push aside my overactive imagination with regard to pockets of pee in the pool. For the first time in a long time I was having a ball in a pool, when out of nowhere some overexuberant youngster threw up into the pool in the exact spot where, only seconds before, I had been splashing around. Apparently he had had too much sun and heat for one day, not to mention all the junk food he had probably eaten on his vacation. Anyway, he did what no one else had been able to do all day: rekindle my dreaded memories of public pools. As well as clear the pool—everyone made a mad dash for the deck, fleeing the floating vomit.

A hotel worker sauntered out with a roll of what looked like police tape, which he threaded haphazardly between the lounge chairs to block off the pool, making it look like a crime scene and attracting curious looks from those passing by. Then the same worker, a kid of no more than eighteen by my estimation, started to tinker with some little vials of something, no doubt to check the level of the chemicals in the pool and determine the exact level of contamination. The worker's age did nothing to reassure me about the cleaning process.

I know they closed the pool for the day, because I kept a close eye on it for the rest of the afternoon and evening. But I can say with some confidence that they never drained the water from the pool and scrubbed it out really well, as we would have done at home after someone had thrown up, say, in the bathtub. The next day the yellow tape was removed and, miraculously, the water was deemed as good as new. Dozens of people were right back in that pool.

I myself didn't return to the pool on that particular vacation. I was, needless to say, deeply suspicious of the whole incident. I was uncertain that that pool was ever really clean. I was starting to think that pool workers just add enough chemicals to neutralize anything floating in the pool; they add enough chemicals to kill the vomit, but not quite enough to harm a small child. Or so they would have us believe.

As I got older, education expanded my knowledge and my imagination became more sophisticated. I learned about bacteria. The more I learned, the more leery I became of any sort of water facility. Wild imaginings, I'm sure, but nevertheless enough to give me an uneasy feeling. There were more than the obvious things, like pee and vomit, to be wary of. Now there were microscopic organisms—things unseen by the naked eye.

I realized that we were lucky to have this water park practically in our backyard; that there were whole communities of people who would have killed for a water facility of any kind, let alone one of this calibre—a world-class facility that would be available for their own use, as well as draw tourists and people from neighbouring areas into their midst, visitors

115

who would bring their money with them and breathe life into the community.

But as I have already mentioned, public pools of any kind, big or small, always make me think of pee, vomit, and bacteria, and this was one big public pool. I was sure it was a breeding ground for all types of vermin, insects, and microscopic scavengers—and now, of course, I could add cockroaches to my list of things to fear at the public pool.

* * * * *

The water park was packed, crawling with people who were out for a day with their family, as our little caravan made its way into the water park in search of a place to set up camp. It was important to have a base camp in a place this size, just in case you were inadvertently separated from your family. Then at least you would have a fixed location where you could regroup.

Our search for four chairs fell short, and so we had to settle for one chair to be home to all our belongings. We piled towels and bags high on that chair as we readied ourselves for the water and our first sliding adventure.

It was at this critical point that I would be forced to remove my T-shirt and sprint for the water. As a courtesy to the other swimmers, so as not to incite a riot or stage a scene out of *Fright*

116

Night, I always wear a T-shirt over my bathing suit right up until the last minute, when I quickly shed the T-shirt and plunge into the water. Don't get me wrong here. I look fine, if fine describes the way you look after two healthy pregnancies, all the while eating plenty of food to nourish those developing babies, and then not getting around to that exercise schedule right after they were born. Or ever, for that matter.

"Maybe when they go to college I'll have time to exercise," I would joke with my friends.

In all honesty, it is unfair of me to blame my lacking body definition on my children. If the truth be known—and I have the pictures to prove it—I wasn't all that physically fit even before I had my children.

But I digress—as the T-shirt came off, my younger daughter Amy, with her freshly scraped knee, stared at my arm.

"What's that on your arm, Mommy?" she said to me.

Now, I have been known to be a little squeamish, and my built-up anxiety—along with all that talk and my own private thoughts about those filthy cockroaches—probably set me off. I immediately assumed that something was crawling on my arm, and of course the creature of choice was none other

117

than the much thought-about cockroach. I launched into the dance of the cockroach, flailing about wildly, trying to flick the disease-infested critter off me, all the while screaming hysterically.

"Get it off! Get it off! Somebody get it off of me! Is it off? Is it off?"

Both my children watched in horror, trying to comprehend what could possibly be wrong with their mother. My husband, on the other hand, my knight in shining armour, went out of his way to pretend he was with another family. Any other family would do; one he could blend in with, preferably one that didn't include a hysterical wife.

"Get it off!" I shrieked, contorting myself in an effort to reach the unknown crawler.

"Off-off-off!" I screamed.

"Why are you screaming, Mommy? There's nothing on your arm," my older daughter Megan finally declared.

So naturally I stopped the dance of the cockroach and tried to look normal for the small group of people who had halted their activity to watch the crazy lady walk the tightrope that stretches over the valley of insanity.

"I meant that line, Mommy," said Amy, pointing to my bicep and the thin scar that ran about four inches across it.

"Oh, that," I gasped, for I was completely out of breath from my near brush with a diseased cockroach.

"It's just a scar I got from some barbed wire when I was a kid," I explained as I huffed and puffed, trying to compose myself.

I hadn't looked at that scar for a long time, and it really took me back to when I was a kid.

*   *   *   *   *

We lived across the street from a big ravine that had a golf course below. All around the perimeter of this golf course was a barbed-wire fence about four feet tall. I knew better than to play on a barbed-wire fence. I had been told plenty of times by my parents; but then, everyone knows that when we're children, we don't always do as we're told. And so one day, against the advice of my parents and my own better judgment, I decided that I could climb that fence. And climb it I did—right up until the time it grabbed hold of my left arm and took its payment, a pound of flesh, for trespassing.

*   *   *   *   *

"Did you have to go to the hospital?" Amy asked wide-eyed, bringing me back from my childhood memory.

"Well, actually, I didn't go to the hospital," I said.

"Really?" said Amy.

119

"I probably should have gone to the hospital and got some stitches, but I never went. I don't think I even went to the doctor. I think Nanna just cleaned it up and put Mercurochrome on it," I continued.

"What's Mercurochrome?" Megan asked.

"Oh, Mercurochrome," and I smiled at the thought, "Nanna loved to use Mercurochrome. It was this orange liquid that was some sort of disinfectant. You rubbed it on the injury, and it turned your skin a bright orange colour and supposedly prevented infection."

"It made your skin bright orange forever?" Megan asked.

"No, not forever, buddy, but for a few days anyway. Nanna thought it was the cure for everything," I said, and I laughed at the thought of my body, a paint-by-number work-in-progress with only the orange filled in, bright orange blotches from being rubbed down with Mercurochrome every summer as a child.

"You mean you were hurt and Nanna and Pa didn't take you to the doctor?" Amy questioned.

Out of the mouths of babes, I thought to myself.

"No, buddy, I guess they didn't."

There was a long pause and what appeared to be a great deal of thought and it was followed by a very logical question from a child.

"If I was with Nanna and Pa and I hurt myself on barbed wire would they take me to the doctor?" Amy questioned.

Amy was very serious, and I knew that this was important to her. I had somehow made her look at her Nanna and Pa in a different way. The Nanna and Pa she knew took you to the doctor for everything. They were not the Mom and Dad I knew. Today they were overcautious to say the least. Either one of their grandchildren needed only to have the slightest sniffle or the littlest scrape, and Nanna and Pa would whisk them off to a medical facility in record time.

"I can say without a doubt they would, buddy, they absolutely would. In fact, I bet they would take you to the doctor even if you didn't need to go."

And I knew that to be true, because after all their Nanna and Pa were not the same Mom and Dad who had raised me: not the same people who worked hard at their jobs every day, not the same people who had rules about the way things should be done, not the same people who had slapped some Mercurochrome on me and told me to suck it up, not the same people who had believed that holidays without their children were a good idea. No, they were Nanna and Pa, the instigators of trouble, the source of unlimited cash, the forgivers of everything, the people whose house you went to for

121

fun and games. Nanna and Pa's grandchildren would never have scars from a barbed-wire fence, they would never need stitches for falling on the razor-sharp coffee table, they would never fall on a junk pile and jab a nail into their knee—but those are different stories.

"Mommy, my leg really hurts where I fell. Maybe I should go to the doctor," Amy said.

I glanced at the cut on Amy's leg.

"Oh, I think you'll be okay, buddy. We'll put some Polysporin on it when we get home."

Nanna and Pa's grandchildren would be free from breaks, bruises, and scars, unless of course their parents were in charge that day.

Perfect love sometimes
does not come until the grandchild.

-Welsh Proverb

THE SHOWDOWN

Some may have called it a showdown, or perhaps a test of wills, me against them. I just called it torture—undue punishment. Why would my parents, whom I adored, do this to me?

I was at the kitchen table staring at a huge hunk of liver: a flat, dense piece of fried internal organ. It was lying beside a mound of mashed potatoes on a dinner plate, my dinner plate, next to my half-empty glass of milk. I had eaten everything else that Mom had put on my plate. My salad, my vegetables—the things that I could eat—were all gone. Oh, I would have eaten the mashed potatoes and finished the milk a long time ago too, but I knew I would need them later. They were going to mask the disgusting texture and taste of liver. I was not a stranger to this showdown. I had been here before; too many times before, in fact—whenever my mother decided it was time for the family to have "a good feed of liver, to get your much-needed iron and all the other valuable minerals", as she so eloquently put it.

For me it was showdown time.

*   *   *   *   *

"I was just hungry for a good feed of liver tonight," my mom would say as our family congregated at the dinner table.

Not that the dinner menu was a surprise; anyone with a nose could smell the stench of frying liver and onions throughout the entire house. So strong and overwhelming was the odour that engulfed our house, it had driven me to spend the last ten minutes in my room mentally preparing myself for the inevitable confrontation.

Mom looked so happy, and she hummed an upbeat tune as she carefully dished up each person's plate. It was not one of those meals where you could decide on the size of your portion; Mom, the liver lover, knew liver was good for you, and she made sure everyone got a healthy share. However, liver didn't bother anyone else in our family. They all dug into their meal with great enthusiasm.

"Great meal!" Dad would say, singing the praises

of the liver, reinforcing Mom's dinner-planning, and ensuring that liver would be on the menu again next week.

"Oh yeah, good salad, Mom," I would add, trying to bank a few points that I would need to use later.

I would always eat my salad—a healthy portion by anyone's standard—and then I would pick away at the vegetables, all the while cutting up my liver into ever-smaller pieces and pushing them around on my plate. About the time that everyone else had finished eating and started clearing the table, I would make my move.

"Thanks for dinner, may I be excused," I would mutter so as not to draw too much attention to myself. And then I would slowly push away from the table—only to be busted before my butt could even get off the chair.

"Kelly, you haven't eaten any of your liver," Mom would state. The tone of her voice and the look on her face was one of shock and disbelief. It was the same look I got after every liver dinner.

"I did, Mom. I had a little," I would lie.

"I think you should finish it. They say that liver is supposed to be very good for you," Mom would counter.

They? Who is *they*, I wanted to ask, and why is it good for you? What does it do, exactly? But I was already on the lower end of this struggle—she being the mother, the big grown-up at the top of the hierarchy; and I being the daughter, the little kid on the bottom. The only one lower on the family totem pole was the family dog, and she ate everything that was thrown at her.

I tried to reason with Mom.

"I don't really like liver, Mom. You know that. It makes me gag," I pleaded, looking for mercy. Of course, there was none.

"Eat your liver, Kelly. You're not leaving this table until you do," she stated with a certain air of finality in her voice.

So there it was, the statement that always led us to the showdown, the battle of the wills.

I sat there for a long time looking at my plate of liver; that unappetizing, dead, and now cold internal organ, with little beads of fat that had congealed and turned white. Then I cut a very small piece off one of the already-cut pieces. I tried to cut it small enough that I could swallow the whole piece without chewing. I buried it in a little coffin of mashed potatoes. Maybe I could fool my taste buds, lead them to believe that only mashed potatoes were coming their way.

I warily picked up the mashed potatoes with the carefully entombed piece of liver and put it into my mouth. So far, so good. Now, if I could just swallow without chewing, I might not taste it at all. But as soon as the food hit my mouth, the instinct to chew was so strong that without thinking I bit into the liver. Swallow, I thought, you just need to swallow! It was then that my gag reflex started working overtime. Milk, I thought frantically, wash it down with milk! I reached for the milk and took a big gulp, using up at least a third of my reserves. I would never have enough milk at this rate; there probably wasn't enough milk in the free world to get me through this meal. Swoosh, down went the liver and the potatoes, followed by a quick milk chaser. A small gag encore, and bite number one was history.

On to bite number two. I fired another tiny piece of liver, encased by potatoes, into my mouth. Don't chew, don't chew, I kept reminding myself. But this time the taste buds were on to me—they knew what to expect. The gag reflex came sooner, and I was too slow with the milk. Back up came the small piece of liver, right back onto the plate. I found it a little amusing that the liver looked pretty much the same coming up as it looked going down. A slight grin crossed my face. Definitely an error during a showdown.

"Do you think that's funny, spitting your food back up onto your plate?" Mom sputtered. "There are children in this world who are starving, you know, and here you are, spitting up a perfectly good meal. Well, you can spit it up all you like. You are still going to eat it!" She was not trying to hide her displeasure with my little show.

*   *   *   *   *

It's a horrible thing to force children to eat their food. And yet I do it myself, today, with my children. Not liver, of course; I would never force my children to eat their liver, or anyone else's for that matter. But then, it's not something you have to worry about in my house, because liver would certainly never be on the menu for one of my meals. I do, however, force them to eat their vegetables; in fact, we usually require a certain number of vegetables, the number varying with the type of vegetable. I do that only because *they* say vegetables are the most important component in a balanced meal. You remember *they,* don't you? Probably the same *they* that told my mom that liver was good for you. Strange how *they* have never grown old and are still around today.

The greatest change in the past thirty-five years, though, is not in what *they* say is good for you. It's in my mother. And I know this to be true because, as I sit here today, at my mother's house for dinner, getting ready to eat the delicious sweet-and-sour pork ribs that my mom makes from scratch, I am witnessing a scene and a conversation straight from *The Twilight Zone.*

"Those smell really good, Mom," I say to my mother as she places a roaster full of ribs in the middle of the table before sitting down at her place.

"I don't like those," says Megan, who is about five, to no one in particular, causing my mom to bounce up like a jack-in-a-box from her chair.

"Mom, sit down," I say quickly. "Megan can try the ribs."

And I turn to Megan and say, "You have never even tried them!"

"But I know I don't like them," Megan counters, looking away from me and toward her nanna, apparently the more sympathetic listener in the room.

"I don't like them either," Amy, the two-year-old, chimes in, following her sister's lead.

"Neither of you has ever had sweet-and-sour pork ribs. At least try one before you say you don't like them," I said.

"It's all right," says my mom, walking back into the kitchen. "Don't force them. They don't have to eat ribs if they don't like them. Now, what would you girls like instead?"

"I would like Kraft Dinner," says Amy.

"I don't want Kraft Dinner. I want a grilled cheese sandwich," says Megan.

And before the girls are even finished with their orders, my mom has the frying pan heating up and a potful of water starting to boil. I can feel the heat escaping from the meal that has already been placed on the table, as we wait for the noodles to boil and the sandwich to grill.

Now I must be in an episode of *Candid Camera,* and at any moment Allen Funt is going to jump out, exposing this scenario as a bad joke that has just been played on me. But there is no joke, and our family dinner finally gets underway more than a little late because my mom, the girls' nanna, had to stop at the onset of our meal to make Kraft Dinner and a grilled cheese sandwich.

When our dinner resumes, it is relatively peaceful. And why shouldn't it be? The girls got exactly what they wanted. As I take my first bite of cold sweet-and-sour ribs and even colder mashed potatoes, I look at my children—they are thoroughly enjoying their piping-hot Kraft Dinner and grilled cheese sandwich.

Yes, having dinner at Nanna's house today reminds me of a scene from the good old days when I was a child. But not really.

131

The reason grandchildren and grandparents get along so well is that they have a common enemy.

-Sam Levenson

THE MAGIC OF THEATRE

Out the window of the airplane I caught a glimpse of the Statue of Liberty. I was bursting with excitement, about to embark on my week-long mother-and-daughter adventure in New York City.

"Look, Megan, look! There's Ellis Island and the Statue of Liberty," I said.

Megan and I had been planning this trip to New York for more than a year. For me New York City is a place like no other—the restaurants, the shopping, the architecture, and of course the theatre. Theatre has long been a passion in my life. Some of my most memorable experiences have occurred in the theatre, whether as a participant or as a spectator.

I couldn't wait to share with Megan the opulence of Broadway theatre. I had been to New York on two previous occasions to take in some Broadway shows with students in my high-school drama classes. But this was the first time I would be sharing the experience with one of my own children.

Megan was only a toddler when Disney released its movie *The Lion King* and, like most youngsters, she fell in love with some of the characters while being frightened of others. She was enchanted by the film. When she was a preschooler, a stuffed Simba and Nala presided over her room atop the pillows at the head of her bed. Her *Lion King* nightlight cast a calming glow day and night. A *Lion King* lamp on her night table illuminated all our bedtime stories about the animals of the Pride Lands. And a precious *Lion King* music box had been gently placed in the centre of the dresser, making music as rich as Elton John himself. A trunk hidden in the far depths of our basement caged a large stuffed Scar, the loathsome *Lion King* villain. Scar was kept locked up in the basement, banished from sight, because Megan didn't want him in her bedroom.

Megan has outgrown all of these children's toys in recent years, and most of them have fallen by the wayside—except for the fragile music box, which was returned to its protective case and is now stored in her closet. She has even overcome her fear of Scar, and he is no longer banished to the basement.

But she still fondly remembers the story of *The Lion King* and all its characters.

On one of my visits to New York I had been fortunate enough to see the Broadway musical of *The Lion King,* and I was barely able to contain my excitement the night Megan and I entered the New Amsterdam Theatre, home to that Tony Award-winning production. Built in 1903 and completely restored in 1997, the New Amsterdam Theatre is considered by some to be the crown jewel of Broadway. It was the perfect place to introduce Megan to Broadway theatre.

My heart started to beat faster before we had even taken our seats. And what great seats they were: fifth row in the orchestra, dead centre. I had purchased our tickets nearly a year in advance, to be sure of getting the best seats in the house.

As the theatre darkened I knew what to expect, and I turned Megan's attention to the aisles of the theatre. As the lights came up, she watched the cast of *The Lion King*—costumed as African elephants, giraffes, cheetahs, gazelles, and exotic birds—present themselves in the aisles and on the stage of the majestic New Amsterdam Theatre.

Megan was mesmerized from the onset. Her eyes were riveted on the show; and my eyes were riveted on her, as if, through her awe at seeing this theatrical wonder for the first time, I could relive my own experience. *The Lion King* did not disappoint. Its smorgasbord of costuming and sets was a feast for the visual palate. It was a masterpiece from beginning to end.

*   *   *   *   *

Even as a child, long before I had any formal schooling in drama, I loved a good stage show. Most of our family get-togethers over the years ended with one show or another that I would stage for the adults. Whether it was a re-enactment of the birth of Jesus or a skit depicting my aunt's weak bladder on her family's long car trips, a good production was always job one in my opinion. I would spend most of the visit scrounging around in my relatives' basements for props and costumes that would jazz up the production, as well as motivating my cousins to try and stage the best production possible.

I always thought of my forceful encouragement as efforts to help my cousins grow into better performers, but to my cousins I was just plain bossy. There is a fine line between being motivational and being bossy, and according to my cousins I crossed that line every time. It was always for love of the stage, though—trying to produce a fine piece of theatre, bigger and better than the time before.

136

When I finished university and became a drama teacher, I experienced the excitement of theatre through my students. Never was I more proud of a group of students than when they wrote and directed a show that won at the zone level and then went on to wow audiences at the provincial festival.

My introduction to professional theatre came late in my teens; in Grade Twelve, to be exact. I remember the experience as if it were yesterday.

*   *   *   *   *

My mom was really excited about an article she had read in the *Edmonton Journal*. She couldn't wait to tell my dad when he came home after work. Fortunately I was there to witness the scene.

"Bob, did you see the *Journal* this morning?" my mom asked my dad.

"I did. Should I have been looking for something in particular?" my dad replied.

"Guess who's doing a show at that dinner theatre at the Mayfield," said Mom.

"I have no idea," replied my dad.

It was easy to see that my dad was not a big fan of live theatre. He didn't even try to muster up any fake enthusiasm for Mom's big news.

"Tab Hunter!" Mom exclaimed excitedly. "Tab Hunter's here in Edmonton, and he's starring in the show at the Mayfield Dinner Theatre."

"Really! I heard the food is very good at that dinner theatre," said Dad.

Mom saw her moment and she took it.

My dad was always keen for a good meal. My mom often referred to his love of food as an obsession, and if you define *obsess* as "to haunt or excessively preoccupy the mind of", then she was right—he was obsessed. But if food was her way into the Mayfield Dinner Theatre to see Tab Hunter, then she was going to grab Dad's obsession and run with it.

"The food there is very good," she said. "Let's go."

How she knew that the food was good is beyond me, for as far as I knew she had never been to the Mayfield Dinner Theatre. I was convinced this was just Mom's way of using Dad's stomach to accomplish her goal—to see Tab Hunter.

None of us had ever been to the Mayfield Dinner Theatre, or to any dinner theatre for that matter. It was strange that we had never been to the Mayfield Dinner Theatre, because when we had first moved to Edmonton and were waiting for our house to be finished, we had lived for two months at the Mayfield Inn, the same hotel that housed the dinner theatre. We could have gone to the Mayfield Dinner Theatre any night of the week during our stay. There would have been no driving, no parking, no checking our coats—just a nice stroll from our room, through the lobby, and down the hall. We never made it that far, though. Somehow we only ever made it as far as Alice's Restaurant or the all-you-can-eat seafood buffet. We did eat numerous meals there. Dad would have been happy to frequent the all-you-can-eat seafood buffet every day. Lucky for me, the Mayfield didn't offer the buffet every day.

Theatre was not at the top of my dad's list of things to do, but if food was thrown into the mix, he might give it a chance.

"Tab Hunter, you say. I haven't heard that name for a long time," my dad said.

Tab Hunter, I thought to myself. I've *never* heard of him.

"Who's Tab Hunter?" I asked them both.

"Oh! Tab Hunter was a huge movie star in the fifties," my mom said. "He starred in lots of movies. He was in *Damn Yankees*. He was a big heartthrob."

Then she smiled and sighed at what I could only assume was the thought of Tab Hunter, the big heartthrob.

"A big movie star is at an Edmonton dinner theatre?" I said with more than a little skepticism. "I doubt it."

"No, really! He even had a number one song. Bob, what was the name of that song he was famous for?" my mom asked.

139

"I think it was 'Young Love', but don't quote me. It was a long time ago," Dad said.

"Bob, we should get tickets and go. We could show Kelly what a big heartthrob from the fifties looks like," said Mom.

And so my introduction to live professional theatre was underway. My mom was so excited that she was going to see Tab Hunter up close and personal that she couldn't wait; she immediately booked tickets to the Sunday matinee. My mom, Mrs. Let's-Find-A-Deal, always gets the best price. Well, the matinee was the best deal and the cheapest price. I don't think Mom mentioned to my dad that the menu for the Sunday brunch wasn't the same as the menu for the evening meals and that's why it was cheaper. The Sunday brunch was no all-you-can-eat seafood buffet, that's for sure. And to say it was "cheaper" needs clarification, because even the matinee was not what either of my parents considered cheap.

I can't say in all honesty that it was a great show. If the truth be known, I don't remember the show at all—not the title, not the main character's name, not the plot. I do remember the experience: the hush as the lights went out; the momentary silence in the darkness as the entire audience waited for whatever would happen next.

What I remember most, however, is that the best deal in the house, the cheapest price, had definite drawbacks.

Our seats were at the back of the theatre and as far off to one side as you could get. I might as well have been trying to see the stage from the lobby. The angle of the table made it impossible for half of us to see the stage. Our chairs were facing the wrong direction, so I was forced to turn my chair as far as possible and then crank my neck the rest of the way. Not a comfortable position for watching two hours of live theatre. During the meal, long before the show started, I complained to my mother.

"Mom, I can't see the stage that well from here. Can we see if the waiter will move us to a better seat, closer to the front?" I asked. "Maybe we could sit at one of those empty tables right near the front."

"Excuse me!" Mom called, beckoning the waiter over to our table. "Could we possibly move to a different table? Maybe one of the empty tables closer to the front?"

"I'm sorry, madam, you have to sit in the seats that you purchased," he said.

I remember thinking that he sounded sort of snobby; but then, what did I know? I was just a teenager in high school and had yet to be exposed to what real snobbery was.

Yes, Mom had bought tickets closer to the back and off to the side because, of course, they were less expensive. What we all found out that day was that when you went to see a big movie star and you bought the cheap seats, you got exactly what you paid for. You didn't get to move up to the more expensive seats the way you would at a sporting event, even if the more expensive seats were empty.

When I look back on it today, I think maybe I've become a bit of a theatre snob myself. I am very picky about where I sit. If I can't get good tickets—in the middle, close to the front—then I don't even want to go; most of the time I won't go. At the time of Tab Hunter's dinner theatre show, however, I had not developed my discriminating tastes, and so I was just glad to have been invited along.

I do remember thinking: Was this guy really a heartthrob in the fifties? I'm not seeing it. Maybe it was the distance from the stage and the skewed angle of my chair, or the kink in my neck, but good old Tab Hunter, the heartthrob from the fifties, wasn't doing anything for me. Maybe it was the fact that I was looking at him in the early eighties. After all, he had been a heartthrob nearly thirty years ago. A lot can happen in thirty years.

And not just to Tab Hunter.

*   *   *   *   *

"Bob, I read in the paper this morning that *Annie* is coming to the Mayfield Dinner Theatre," Mom said one day.

"Really? I haven't been to the Mayfield Dinner Theatre in years. I heard the food there is pretty good," said Dad.

I wanted to laugh out loud. "Hadn't been there in years" was an understatement. He hadn't been there since Tab Hunter was the headliner and I was in Grade Twelve.

"Bob, let's take Megan and Amy to a dinner show at the Mayfield," said my mom.

"Well, let's go to the evening show. I heard the food then is really good, better than at the matinee," Dad replied.

"Mom, Megan and Amy are pretty young to go to the Mayfield," I said.

"No, *Annie* will be a great show for the girls," Mom countered.

Unlike Mom and Dad, the non-theatre people in our family, I had been to the Mayfield Dinner Theatre a few times since the Tab Hunter show, and

I knew a little bit about the Theatre, including the prices.

"I don't mean the show is too old for them, Mom," I said. "I mean Amy is only four, and the dinner theatre doesn't have a price for children. You're going to pay about sixty dollars for each ticket, and you'll be lucky if the girls eat two dollars' worth of food between them," I said, trying to reason with her.

"That doesn't matter," Mom said, "as long as they want to go."

"And Martha," my dad said to my mom, "make sure you get tickets in the centre and up near the front, so the girls won't have any trouble seeing the stage."

"Kelly, maybe you can come with me when I buy the tickets, and you can show me which seats would be the best for the girls, since you know all about that stuff," Mom said.

And so for the past eight years I have been selecting the tickets for my mom and dad to take their granddaughters to dozens of musical productions, dinner theatres, and stage shows, because apparently in my parents' eyes I know the most about great seat selection.

Tab Hunter didn't look much like a heartthrob in the 1980s, thirty years after his booming movie career. And thirty years after the 1980s Nanna and

Pa don't look much like my mom and dad either. They have even become patrons of the arts. And the most surprising part of all is that now they are paying the extra money and getting the good seats.

Isn't it wonderful what grandchildren can open your eyes to.

The simplest toy,
one even the youngster can operate,
is called a grandparent.

-Sam Levenson

CROSSING CENTRE STREET

The clock showed it was early, only seconds after 7:55 a.m. The late April sun was already well into the sky. The warmth of the sun was a welcome change from the darkness that had been greeting me for so many months. It was not early for some, I'm sure; but to me, barely eight years old, 7:55 a.m. seemed very early. Granted, it was my regular time to leave the house, to head out to school. But I don't do mornings well—never have, never will.

I was wearing my favourite outfit, featuring a pair of purple plaid polyester pants. They were a little too short, hovering just above my ankle bones and sometimes the victim of the where's-the-flood joke. They were held in place with an elastic waistband that was a little too snug, leaving a bumpy ridge on the skin around my waist. But I loved those pants, and I thought they looked terrific on me. I had another pair, exactly the same except that they were pink plaid. They were my second-favourite pair of pants. Even at the age of eight I wasn't a lover of shopping; and I believed that when you found a fashion piece that worked for you, you should buy one in every colour. That was my purchasing philosophy at age eight, and it remains my purchasing philosophy some thirty-five years later.

To put the finishing touches on my outfit, I wore a white Phentex poncho, complete with dangling fringe that hung down just below the waistband of the pants, and a matching white Phentex tam. My grandmother had crocheted them especially for me.

Phentex is not a word you hear very often anymore, but you might recall the seventies, when it was very popular with grandmothers. You could buy Phentex like wool, in skeins or balls. You could knit with it or, as in the case of my poncho and tam, crochet with it. My grandmother made numerous things from wool; and she made a variety of things with Phentex too, everything from clothing to the little dolls that sit on toilet tanks with rolls of toilet paper hidden in their skirts. However, that was where the similarities between wool and Phentex ended. There is absolutely no natural fibre in Phentex. I'm sure that, if you stood too close to an open flame, Phentex would melt onto your skin.

Looking back, I can see that my purple plaid, polyester, and Phentex outfit was entirely hideous, but on that morning I was as pleased as punch to be wearing it. I checked myself out one final time in the bathroom mirror: The plaid pants looked fabulous, and the white Phentex glistened in the light. The poncho had been crocheted with just the right tension, letting a hint of the colour through from the lavender shirt and the purple plaid pants.

Never was there a more hip outfit in a Grade Three classroom. I knew I would be the envy of all the other girls. They would beg to try on my stylish Phentex poncho and tam. In my mind I identified with Mary Tyler Moore, wearing her poncho as she crossed the road at the beginning of every *Mary Tyler Moore* show. She would always pause in the middle of the street and toss her tam into the air, declaring her independence to the world. I couldn't wait to cross Centre Street today, knowing I would be channeling Mary Tyler Moore's energy—although I wouldn't dare toss my tam into the air for fear of getting it dirty or, worse yet, losing it in the traffic.

Normally I was a little frightened to cross Centre Street by myself. Even though I had been riding the

Calgary city buses alone and crossing Centre Street solo for the entire school year, I still felt a little anxiety every day when I stuck my neck out into the oncoming traffic. It was difficult to find a break in the traffic. The daily commuters—the maniacs who used this thoroughfare twice daily for their journey to and from work—drove with reckless abandon. To an eight-year-old it felt like facing a barrage of artillery shells every morning. Calgary was a far cry from the small Alberta town where we had lived only a year ago, where I could walk to school every day and never worry about traffic.

My dad was excited when we moved to the big city. He had sold me on the move by talking up the fact that I would never have to walk to school again. In the city I would just jump onto a school bus—a bus filled with other students, my new best friends—that would pick me up at my front door and drop me off right at the doors of the school. It had sounded good in theory, but the facts of the matter were quite different. I did not ride a school bus. The city bus that I rode did not pick me up at my front door; I had to hoof it down the street a whole block and a half to catch it. And it was not filled with students, my new best friends. There were no students on the bus at all—only adults on their way downtown to their jobs, old grumpy people who never spoke. As for friends, my only best friend on the bus was the bus driver. Furthermore, the city bus did not stop in front of my school. No, it stopped on the other side of Centre Street, which I had to risk my life crossing every morning without the benefit of street lights, playing chicken with the daily commuters as they raced to get downtown.

I was pretty much on my own in the mornings before leaving for the bus. My dad left for work in what seemed to me like the wee hours of the morning; usually he was gone before I was even out of bed. At 7:55 my mom would be finishing up the last touches on her hair and makeup, and then she too would be on her way to the office.

Today, after checking myself out one last time in the bathroom mirror, I said a quick goodbye to Mom and headed out through the kitchen, grabbing my Flintstones lunch box that was packed and waiting for me on the counter.

I was pleased with the acquisition of my Flintstones lunch box. I had really wanted that particular lunch box, and I distinctly remember arguing my case with Mom and Dad. A well-constructed lunch box was important, I told them, due to my long daily commute to school on the city bus.

The lunch box itself was a masterpiece, with a

beautifully drawn picture of Fred and the gang on the lid. The picture was even embossed, and the layered picture made the lunch box look extra-fancy. Little metal buckles snapped shut to hold the lid firmly in place, and a little clasp on the inside held the Thermos snug at one end, protecting the rest of the lunch from being crushed by the force of the Thermos rolling around inside. As I proudly carried my Flintstones lunch box out the front door, I pictured the treasures of my midday meal hidden inside, as well as the tasty drink in my Fred-and-the-gang Thermos. I walked with great confidence down the slope of our yard and onto the sidewalk. I knew I was a fashion trend-setter, strutting along in my favourite outfit, sporting the accessory to beat all accessories, the Flintstones lunch box.

Today I was looking forward to catching that bus and riding it those twenty-seven city blocks down Centre Street to the main intersection, where I would cross Centre Street and stride with confidence up the hill to St. Paul Catholic Elementary School. Everyone on that bus—regular riders that I saw every day and travellers who were new to this bus route—would silently approve of my outfit; in twenty-seven blocks a whole variety of people would get to view my fashion debut. Not to mention the bus driver; he always had a thoughtful comment for me, the little girl who braved the Centre Street bus all alone every day.

As I walked toward Centre Street I could see the bus pull up to the bus stop. I was still about a hundred yards away, and I quickened my pace as the front door of the bus opened. I wasn't afraid that the bus driver would leave without me; I knew from past experience that he wouldn't. I was fairly certain I was his favourite passenger. He always waited when he could see me and Fred and the gang coming down the street toward the bus.

In my eagerness to get to the bus and show off my outfit, however, I started running; just lightly at first and then full force, swinging my Flintstones lunch box back and forth and bouncing it against my leg as I headed for the bus and, ultimately, my date with the fashion hall of fame. While I was running I felt the Thermos bottle suddenly shift inside the lunch box, smashing into the helpless treats that were now victims of the loose Thermos running wild inside the lunch box. I glanced toward my lunch box, taking my eyes off the sidewalk for a split second.

It was then that disaster struck—as it always does, just when you least expect it. The sidewalk had heaved just a little in one spot, and in my haste and lack of focus I caught my toe and I tripped. I lost my balance just enough to be propelled slightly forward, out of control. I fought a good fight to rectify my course, but to no avail. Within seconds I totally lost my balance and, in order to save my face, I flung my arms out in front of me, letting go of my treasured Flintstones lunch box.

The rest seemed to take place in slow motion.

It was immediately obvious that I didn't just drop my lunch box. I actually tossed it into the air. Perhaps the buckles securing the lid of Fred-and-the-gang to the box were not fastened properly, or else the jostling of the Thermos had sprung the lid. In any case, as the lunch box rose heavenward, the lid flipped open and the contents of my midday meal flew out in every direction. The little clasp that had been holding the Thermos in place now flapped in the air as if waving goodbye, freeing the Thermos to sail through the air before smashing onto the ground with enough force to shatter the glass interior and render it useless. I watched helplessly as my drink seeped from the cracked lid, staining the sidewalk bright red. It must have been cherry Kool-Aid, my favourite. Gone was my cherished drink.

My sandwich—my precious peanut-butter-and-honey sandwich, which had been my lunch entree of choice for the past year—did a beautiful loop before landing in a misshapen heap in front of me. At this point I realized something about myself: I was not very good at dodging things while I was flailing out of control. I saw my sandwich on the ground, but I was unable to redirect my step. My left foot pounded down on top of the already squashed sandwich, leaving it an unrecognizable mass inside the little sandwich bag tightly secured with a white and red twist-tie.

I fell forward and slowly skidded on the cement, driving sand and gravel into the palms of my hands. Finally I ground to a stop, thanks in part to the friction of my knees and the knees of my pants against the sidewalk. Blood began to ooze from my hands, as well as from my knees—through rips in my favourite pants.

Lying motionless, stunned, the side of my face plastered to the cement, I was at the perfect angle to watch my orange smash onto the sidewalk. It bounced twice, rolled under a parked car, and came to rest just behind the tire of another parked car. I inched my body over toward the vehicle, remaining flat on my belly in a futile attempt to rescue the citrus portion of my lunch. My arms were just too short to reach underneath that car.

When I finally struggled to my feet, I realized what an error it had been to drag myself across the sidewalk in my white Phentex poncho. The purple plaid pants had also fallen victim to the filth of the road, not that they weren't already ruined from the rips and the blood. My favourite outfit was almost completely destroyed. The only article of clothing that remained intact was the white Phentex tam that had miraculously survived the mishap and was still sitting precariously on my head. I glanced back toward my house with a fleeting hope that Mom might be bolting to my rescue, but Mom's car was no longer parked in front of the house. Apparently she had left for work sometime between my leaving the house and my encounter with the uneven sidewalk.

Looking back toward the bus, I could see that the driver had left his charge and was racing down the street to help me. The passengers from the bus seemed to be watching as I tried to regain my composure. But the thought of all those people watching me in my ruined outfit, the outfit that was to have launched my fashion debut, was more than I could take. I immediately started to cry. The bus driver reached me as the first tears fell and my nose began to run. As if my torn pants and bleeding kneecaps weren't enough—in an effort to pull myself together, I wiped the tears and the snot with the back of my bleeding hands. With that multicoloured master stroke the final picture of me, a total wreck, seemed complete.

The bus driver gathered up my broken Thermos

and my squished sandwich. He even reached under the car and retrieved my orange, his arms being a fair bit longer than mine. He carefully returned all the items to my lunch box and attempted to close the lid, to hide them behind Fred and the gang. But the impact of the crash had bent the frame of either the lid or the box, or both, and they no longer fit together. He held the lunch box closed as we walked together toward the bus. Curious eyes followed us from every bus window.

I was humiliated as I stepped up into the bus and took the front seat that someone had been kind enough to vacate for me. The bus driver handed me my lunch box and the box of Kleenex that he kept by his seat. I clutched the lunch box to my chest in an effort to hold it closed and comfort myself. I silently cried all the way down Centre Street, all the while using the Kleenex to do a makeshift cleanup of my face. When we reached my stop, the bus driver got up out of his seat for the second time that day and helped me disembark from the front door of the bus. I kept my head low, still clutching my lunch box and hoping no one would see me, as the bus pulled away from the bus stop and headed south, bound for downtown.

I stood on the corner, quite shaken from my humiliating ordeal, and I watched the traffic zoom past me in both directions. For some reason the traffic seemed to be much faster today. It was hard to see a break in the steady stream of vehicles, and I was more afraid than ever to cross this busy intersection by myself. I feared that the drivers would be unable to see me in all my filth, for I was sure that I was the same colour as the dirty street. I tentatively stuck out my right arm, still clutching the warped lunch box in my left. I patiently waited for the traffic to come to a reluctant stop and then stepped out onto the street. Walking across the street—broken lunch box, ripped and bloody pants, dirty white poncho, and face smeared with bodily fluids—I knew for a fact that I no longer resembled Mary Tyler Moore. Except for maybe the tam. Yes, I still had the white tam sitting proudly on my head. I was holding on to my vision of Mary Tyler Moore by a thread, and it was a Phentex thread at that.

My Fred-and-the-gang lunch box never worked quite right after that, and I was reluctant to use it again. In the back of my mind I distrusted it, and worried that it might burst open at any moment.

I noticed recently, some thirty-five years after that fateful day, that you can buy vintage lunch boxes on the Internet. And wouldn't you know, there was a Flintstones lunch box for sale, complete with Thermos and in mint condition of course. The asking price was $760—yes, seven hundred and sixty dollars. Had my parents only known back then, they might have chosen not to let me use that lunch box, but instead have tucked it away to sell at a later date.

But then, many things are more valuable now than they were in the 1970s. Take children, for example: My parents, the same people who sent me off on a city bus to fight the Centre Street traffic when I was in Grade Three, are very concerned that I am considering letting my daughter, who will be in Grade Five, take the school bus next year instead of driving her to school myself. The school bus will stop on our street to pick her up, and it will drop her off directly in front of her school. She will share her bus only with other students from her school and will not be exposed to the general public. She will not have to cross any major intersections; in fact, she won't have to cross any road at all. Yes, it seems that lunch boxes and children have gone way up in value since I was a little girl in the seventies.

THE ALARM

It was a typical day. I had popped in to see my mom and dad. Even though I was a grown woman who had not lived at home for nearly a quarter of a century, that was not an unusual occurrence. I usually see one or both of my parents every day.

But I couldn't believe my eyes when I saw my mom. She looked tired, dead tired. I had never seen my mom look quite this bad. Black bags sagged under puffy eyelids that drooped over her bloodshot eyes. Her posture was slumped as she shuffled through the kitchen. My mom never shuffled; she was always a ball of fire running hither and thither. She didn't seem to have the energy to hold herself upright. It was as if she had gone through some sort of metamorphosis; and overnight, instead of emerging as a beautiful butterfly, she had suddenly become an old woman.

So it was entirely out of concern, not malice, that I mentioned this to her.

"You look horrible, Nanna. Are you feeling okay?" I asked. Since the birth of my children I quite often call my parents Nanna and Pa.

I waited for the response, expecting that Mom would tell me she hadn't slept well because my dad's horrific snoring had kept her awake all night. Both of my parents were masters at blaming each other for their lack of a good night's sleep. It was a good-natured teasing that went on at their house quite often, but this time she didn't blame my dad for her lack of zzzz's the night before.

Her hackles were up, and I could sense that she was ready to do battle as only my mom can. However, for the first time that I could recall, she couldn't muster the energy. Then she simply looked at me (or did she glare?) and I thought I detected just a smidgen of anger being tossed in my direction. For a fleeting moment, I thought she was going to blame me for her fatigue. But how could that be? I hadn't seen her since noon the day before.

"I'm going to lie down," she finally said. "I'm exhausted."

And she turned away and slowly shuffled out of sight.

I was quite sure that she was exhausted. She certainly looked exhausted. If I hadn't known better, I would have thought she had been out on the town the night before, tying one on. But I did know better.

I myself had gone out the previous evening with my husband. We had left our children at home alone together. It was not a big deal; they had stayed alone before, just not late in the evening. Our older daughter was well into junior high school and more than capable of taking care of herself and her younger sister. In fact, she was already babysitting for other people, a job that seemed to be quite lucrative these days. Five dollars an hour per child, tax-free.

Babysitting was starting to look good even to me. It was a far cry from the meagre fifty cents an hour I used to make babysitting in the seventies, and it wasn't fifty cents per child back then. No sir, it was fifty cents an hour for as many kids as they could cram into their house. Some families even pooled their children, bringing them all to one house, where they could share my hefty fee and ease the financial burden.

Knowing that Mom and Dad were planning to be home for the whole evening, I had mentioned to my girls as well as my mom and dad that if the girls ran into any problem they could always phone Nanna and Pa. Apparently that was my first mistake.

"You know, your mom didn't sleep at all last night," said my dad after Mom had walked into the bedroom and not only closed but locked the bedroom door.

"I can see that. What's the problem?" I asked.

I didn't need to ask; I knew he was going to tell me anyway. That is the great thing about our family: nobody holds back, we just say what's on our mind. I guess that on some occasions forthright honesty is the not-so-great thing about our family too.

"Oh, you know your mother—she was worried all night about the girls being home alone," he said.

"The girls were fine, Dad. We were home by midnight. They were both sound asleep when we got home. They are more than old enough to stay home by themselves," I stated.

"I'm sure they are. However, you know your mother—she is never going to be able to sleep when those girls are home by themselves. She's convinced that someone will break into the house while they're home by themselves. She just worries herself sick," he said.

I didn't know where this was going, but my

grandparent sensors were on high alert. It was only a matter of time, I thought to myself, before the shoe drops. I've walked this road before.

"You need to get an alarm. I'm sure she'll sleep better if she knows you have an alarm," Dad said.

And there it was. The big shoe had dropped. Dad was the messenger and that shoe hit the floor like a sledgehammer. It was my fault.

"We have an alarm," I said, and smiled.

"Very funny," he replied. "Now what you really need to do is to get your alarm hooked up. Then your mother *might* be able to sleep at night. However, even with the alarm there is no guarantee."

My husband, my two girls, and I had moved into a new house about a year and a half prior to this conversation. We had an alarm system wired into the house when it was being built; however, I had never gotten around to contacting an alarm company to have it activated.

As I thought about my father's suggestion to have the alarm activated, I couldn't help but think about the new house we had moved into in Calgary when I was a kid, their little girl.

*   *   *   *   *

We had taken possession of the Calgary house when I was in Grade Four and, since my mom worked full-time, she had arranged for me to go to a

165

neighbour's house for lunch and after school. I always wished I had an older brother or sister to go home with at lunch and then again after school. I had decided that being the oldest child in the family had very few benefits.

From watching the interaction of my friends with their older brothers and sisters I saw many advantages of not being the oldest. My friends with older brothers and sisters had far more freedom then I did. They had someone to pave the way, to blaze the trail, to soften up the parents—or just to wear the parents down. I needed an older sibling to teach me all the little survival tricks a kid needed to know.

But when I entered Grade Six, I was liberated. I had argued long and hard, and it was finally agreed, that I was old enough to come home alone for lunch and after school.

There were other things that were changing in my life in Grade Six. I was growing up. In my own eyes I was on the verge of womanhood; however, I was having a hard time convincing Mom and Dad or anyone else of my impending adultness.

I was not alone in my quest for adulthood. I had a number of friends who were trying to beat the clock as well. My friends and I wanted so much to appear grown-up that we decided we would each start to carry a purse. I didn't really need a purse. If the truth be told, I didn't have anything to put in a purse. But in my circle of friends a purse was associated with the world of the adult woman; therefore, I was determined to have a purse and the obvious adult respectability that went with it.

So off to the mall I went, with my mother in tow, to look for my much-desired purse. My choices were limited because I had no money to speak of and my mother was never too quick to part with hers. To Mom's credit, she did participate in the search for the perfect grown-up purse; unfortunately, the search was not successful. Mom and I were unable to agree on either the price or the purse. Mom couldn't get past the cheap little kid purses, and I had my mind set on an expensive grown-up one. We reached an impasse, and we headed home purseless.

Mom was sympathetic to my needs, however, and she found an old purse of hers that she thought might serve the purpose. It was fortunate for me that Mom was always up on the latest styles, and so her recently discarded purse suited my purpose very well. It wasn't new, but I figured that might even work to my advantage. The purse appeared used and would create the impression that I had been carrying a purse for a while, making me appear even older and more womanly.

Once the purse had been acquired, I needed to find items that would be purseworthy. As I was perched on the cusp of adulthood, I knew you couldn't just put any old thing in your purse. Purse articles needed to look important, so that when you nonchalantly pulled them out of the purse in front of a crowd of people, no one would question the legitimacy of the purse. It would be readily apparent that you were grown-up enough to need it.

My grape Lip Smacker seemed an obvious choice to go in the purse. Every one understood the need for Lip Smacker; at least all my friends did, and anyone else who had ever experienced chapped lips. I could easily pull out that Lip Smacker three or four times a day and apply it to my lips. My grape Lip Smacker wasn't one of those itty-bitty Lip Smackers the size of your pinky finger—it was a big fat honker, as big around as a roll of loonies or toonies.

Of course, there were no loonies or toonies then. Back in the seventies we still had the faithful one- and two-dollar bills. I had no bills to put in my purse, so I didn't need a billfold or a wallet. I was content with a little rubber coin purse, the kind that had a slit down the middle, and you needed to squeeze on both ends to get it to open up. My grandfather had a coin purse like that, and I always thought it was the greatest gadget. He kept his coin purse in his pocket, and he told me he had never lost any change from that rubber coin purse. It was sealed tight unless you squeezed on both ends. I had a bit of change that I carefully placed into my rubber coin purse and then put in my bigger purse.

Although there was not an abundance of money in my life, I knew money was always important to carry in your purse. You didn't need to have a large amount of money; usually ten cents, one thin dime, was enough. In my youthful days, long before everyone had a cellphone hanging off their ear, you tried to keep a dime in reserve for the pay phone, to call home in an emergency.

I had no use for money at school. We didn't have any vending machines; they would be a thing of the future. No one stayed for lunch, so there was nothing to buy and no time to buy it. There were no hot lunches, no lunchtime bake sales, no Snack Shack.

Staying for lunch wasn't even an option at the elementary school I went to in the 1970s. If you couldn't go to your own house for lunch, then your parents needed to make arrangements for you to go to someone else's house. Since both Mom and Dad worked, I ate lunch at a neighbour's house every day in Grade Four and Five, until I was old enough to go home by myself. It wasn't until years later that I realized my parents paid our neighbour to feed me. What an eye opener! I always thought she was just a really nice lady because she stayed home to make my lunch.

The first day I came home for lunch by myself was a day like no other. No one had prepared my lunch, so the menu was not predetermined. Some serious thought went into my first solo meal: Mushroom soup was a definite favourite. Tomato soup, delicious with a handful of crushed crackers. Or the old standby, Kraft Dinner. I chose Kraft Dinner. The thought of not having to share with anyone, but being able to eat the whole box myself, was very exciting.

I cooked the meal carefully, having a great respect for the hot element on the stove. I was cautious of the boiling water when I ceremoniously dumped in the noodles. My mom was a pro at making Kraft Dinner. She never timed her noodles—she could sense when they were done—and she certainly never measured out the milk and the butter. I thought I too was a pro when it came to Kraft Dinner. Pros don't need a timer, and they don't need to measure. I had learned that from watching my mother.

It seems I went wrong in a number of critical places. Apparently my noodles needed to cook a little longer, as they were just a little harder than *al dente.* And I inadvertently added too much milk and butter. This left my Kraft Dinner noodles a little on the crunchy side and the cheese sauce a little more soupy than saucy. But even the less-than-perfect Kraft Dinner couldn't dampen this monumental day for me.

I took my hard, soupy noodles and a huge glass of RC Cola into the living room. I was living dangerously. I wasn't allowed to drink pop during the week, but who would be the wiser? Besides, I was already bending all the rules: the one about no eating in the living room, and the one about no watching television while you were eating. (The two rules were redundant really, since the only television was in the living room.) You did not eat in the living room in the Adams house, and you certainly did not watch television during mealtime.

I believe I watched the Flintstones during my fine-dining experience. But the particular show wouldn't have mattered; I would have been elated to watch anything. I ate that whole box of Kraft Dinner on my own and experienced only a slight stomach ache as a result of my gluttony.

Before returning to school, I placed the pot and my bowl and fork in the sink, and I left the milk and butter on the counter. All these actions would be discussed at a later time—when Mom and Dad got home from work that evening, to be exact.

I grew up in a community that had a little man-made lake. If you lived in that community, you had the option of being a member of the lake association. Aside from the lake itself, the facility offered a small skating area where you could take skating lessons in the winter; a great toboggan hill; a couple of tennis courts; a tarmac with eight basketball hoops; and lots of other things to keep you active year-round. Because it was a community lake, you needed to be a member of the lake association to gain admittance.

A chain-link fence about eight feet high ran around the entire perimeter of the facility except for the area where a few houses backed onto the lake. The houses that backed onto the lake were the envy of everyone else in the community. If you weren't fortunate enough to live on the lake, which I wasn't, then you needed an identification card to gain entry at one of the two gated entrances. Every year you got a new picture taken for your lake card, and then they would plasticize it for you so it was hard like a credit card.

I decided that my lake card was something else I could keep in my purse. I didn't really need my lake card at school, but I thought it would be handy if I ever took my purse to the lake.

It was a thrill to be able to also add a house key to the contents of my purse. I didn't want to be one of those kids who had to wear their house key around their neck. They were so obviously latchkey kids. I could be a latchkey kid and no one would know, because my key would be safely tucked away in my purse.

I remember the purse vividly. It had two big, round, plastic handles about the size of small Frisbees. I could put my arm through the handles and push the purse all the way up to my shoulder. Not the way the designer pictured it, I'm sure, but I liked it nonetheless. The body of the purse was lashed onto the handles with some sort of macramé cord that then continued in a knotted pattern to make up the body of the purse. It was lined with fake silk that had started to fray within weeks of the initial purchase, long before Mom gave it to me. The frayed lining was probably the reason my mom quit using the purse and relegated it to me in the first place.

At the outset of my independence I religiously followed an organizational system. I have always been very good at developing and implementing organizational systems; it has generally been in the maintaining of the system where I have fallen short.

I left the house every morning proudly carrying my school books and my purse with my Lip Smacker, my rubber coin purse, my lake card, and my key bouncing around in the big belly of my purse. I would meet up with the girl who lived across the street; and together, with our purses tucked neatly under our arms, we would make our way to school.

When we got to school we would tuck our purses under our desks just like the rest of our grown-up school friends.

I would never think of leaving my purse outside the classroom, on the hook with my jacket. I was worried it would fall victim to the school thief. I didn't know who the school thief was, or if we really had a school thief, but things had been known to go missing from time to time. The fact that there was nothing worth stealing in my purse was irrelevant. I needed my purse to be close at hand. After all, people couldn't see how grown-up I was if I didn't have my purse within reach.

At lunch and at the end of the day I walked home with my purse and the girl who lived across the street, and I used my key to gain entry to our house. The purse and my system worked well for the first couple of days. But, as with many things in my life, everything doesn't always go according to plan.

About the third day I deviated from the original plan. After I returned from school for the lunch hour and entered the house using my key, I placed it on the ledge in the front entrance, instead of returning it to its rightful place in my purse. I was probably in a hurry. My lunch hours were slightly more rushed now that I was required to clean up my mess before I returned to school, and I probably wasn't paying close enough attention to where I had laid down my key. After lunch I absent-mindedly headed back to school without my key.

My afternoon went off without a hitch, right up until I approached my front door at the end of the school day.

My friend from across the street was coming home with me on this particular day. We had talked all day about making a Barbie fortress after school. I liked the freedom of coming home alone, not having to obtain permission to have a friend over and play Barbies.

Not to mention that no one was there to monitor the amount of ice cream we ate for an after-school snack. When I was home alone, I could heap a soup bowl full with ice cream, chocolate sauce, and whipped cream, and no one was the wiser. Eventually Mom did catch on to the amount of ice cream I was going through, but not before I had eaten a small country's share.

As I stood on the front steps of my house and searched the belly of my purse for the key, I quickly got a sick feeling in the pit of my stomach. It didn't take me long to realize my key was not there—the inside of the purse was so empty that a key had few places to hide.

To this day I chuckle at the way young people think. It never occurs to them that they are in a bad position because of their own doing. It certainly never occurred to me. No, it must be someone else that has put them in that position. Taking responsibility is something that people learn over time—with age, or in some cases not at all.

"Oh no!" I said to my friend. "Somebody must have stolen my key out of my purse."

"Don't you have your lake card in your purse?" my friend asked.

"Yes, but I can't go to the lake right now. I have to figure out how to get into my house before Mom and Dad get home," I replied to my friend.

"I know," said my friend. "But you can use your lake card to get into your house."

I had absolutely no idea what she was talking about. She sounded like a lunatic, and I didn't know what to say to a lunatic. So I said nothing; I just stared at her.

"Get your lake card out, and I'll show you," she said.

I tentatively reached back into my purse and fished around for my lake card. I pulled it out of my purse and handed it to her. What she did next was remarkable. With the smoothness of an international jewel thief she slid that plasticized card between the door and the door jamb at precisely the location of the latch, and like magic the door swung open.

"Oh my gosh!" I exclaimed. "Where did you learn to do that?"

"My older brother showed me," she simply stated. "He says you can open all the doors on this street with your lake card. Or any credit card for that matter."

Just another reason for me to wish I had an older brother or sister, I thought. They knew so much cool stuff. I wondered where they got their information. Not that I really cared where the information came from. I just wished I had an older sibling who could share it with me.

"In fact my brother said that since this neighbourhood was developed by the same builder, he can probably open every house in the neighbourhood with a lake card," my friend said. She smiled, pleased with herself that she knew something I didn't.

It never occurred to me to wonder how my friend's brother had stumbled across this information, or to be worried that maybe he and his friends were involved in things that might be unlawful. I didn't even care if her brother could open all the doors on the street. I was just excited to gain entry to my house and wished I had been the one to share the information with my friend instead of the other way around.

"I need to try that," I said.

I went into the house and locked the door, pulling it shut as I came back out onto the front steps. Then I took my lake card and slid it between the door and the door jamb just as I had watched my friend do. Like magic our door opened. So easy that even a child could do it, I thought.

We lived in that house for almost eight years. We never changed the locks or figured out how to fix the whole easy-entry problem. I continued to gain entry to my house using my lake card for as long as we lived there.

On the rare occasion that I forgot both my key and my lake card I would run across the street to a house where I babysat, and I would ask the lady of the house if I could borrow her credit card, and I would use it to gain entry to my house. She knew what I wanted the card for. Everyone laughed about the easy-entry system the builder had provided in our neighbourhood. No one seemed concerned about the risk of someone breaking into their homes. And in fact, for as long as we lived there I don't recall anyone's house ever being robbed.

My mom didn't seem to have trouble with sleepless nights when I was at home alone in that alarm-free house. Or, for that matter, in the next alarm-free house we lived in. I do know it wasn't until after I moved out that Mom and Dad finally had an alarm system hooked up in their house.

Knowing my mother, I would feel safe in betting that she finally had an alarm installed in anticipation of the grandchildren being born. Nothing would surprise me.

Being grandparents sufficiently removes us from the responsibilities so that we can be friends.

-Allan Frome

KELLY HYMANYK

Kelly Hymanyk was born in Calgary, Alberta in 1963. She is a teacher and a freelance writer. 'WHO ARE THESE PEOPLE, AND WHAT HAVE YOU DONE WITH MY PARENTS?' is her first collection of humorous short stories. She currently lives in Edmonton with her husband and two children, only blocks away from her parents.

GIVE A "ROBERT J. ADAMS" OR
"KELLY HYMANYK"
BOOK TO A FRIEND

Megamy Publishing Ltd.
Box 3507
Spruce Grove, AB   T7X 3A7

Send to:
Name:_____

Street:_____

City:_____
Province/   Postal/
State:_____ Zip Code:_____

Please send:

"The Stump Farm"   @ $18.95 =_____

"Beyond the Stump Farm"   @ $18.95 =_____

"Horse Cop"   @ $18.95 =_____

"Fish Cop"   @ $18.95 =_____

"The South Road"   @ $18.95 =_____

"Skunks and Hound Dogs"   @ $18.95 =_____

"In the Shadow of the Rockies"   @ $18.95 =_____

"Dynamite Hill"   @ $18.95 =_____

"I Should've Had My Grandkids First" @ $18.95 =_____

**"Who Are These People and What
  Have You Done With My Parents?"**   @ $18.95 =_____

Shipping and handling per book   @ $ 5.00 =_____

                                         6% GST =_____

                    Total amount enclosed: _____

Make cheque or money order payable to:
Megamy Publishing Ltd.
Price subject to change without prior notice.
ORDERS OUTSIDE OF CANADA must be paid in U.S. funds by cheque or money
order drawn on U.S. or Canadian Bank. Sorry no C.O.D.'s.